The Fundamentals of Interactive Design
Michael Salmond/Gavin Ambrose

academia

An AVA Book

Published by AVA Publishing
50 Bedford Square
London
WC1B 3DP
Tel: +44 0207 631 5600
Email: enquiries@avabooks.com

Distributed by Macmillan Distribution
(ex-North America & Canada)
Brunel Road
Houndmills
Basingstoke
Hants
RG21 6XS
Tel (Home): +44 (0) 1256 302 692
Fax (Home): +44 (0) 1256 812 521
Tel (Export): +44 (0) 1256 329 242
Fax (Export): +44 (0) 1256 842 084

Distributed in the USA & Canada by Macmillan
Orders:
MPS
P.O. Box 470
Gordonsville, VA 22942-8501
Phone: 888-330-8477
Fax: 800-672-2054
Email: orders@mpsvirginia.com

Returns:
MPS Returns Center
14301 Litchfield Drive
Orange, VA 22960
Phone: 888-330-8477

ISBN 978-2-940411-86-3

Library of Congress Cataloging-in-Publication Data
Salmond, Michael; Ambrose, Gavin.
The Fundamentals of Interactive Design / Michael Salmond
and Gavin Ambrose p. cm.
Includes bibliographical references and index.
ISBN: 9782940411863 (pbk.:alk.paper)
eISBN: 9782940447480
1. Computer-aided design. 2. Design -- Technological innovations.
NK1520 .S35 2013

10 9 8 7 6 5 4 3 2 1

Text by Michael Salmond
Design by Gavin Ambrose
Cover image (*The World's Biggest Pac-Man*) by Soap Creative

Production by BMAG Production Mgt. LLP, Singapore
Email: alicegoh@bmag.com.sg

Michael Salmond/Gavin Ambrose

The Fundamentals of Interactive Design

Ethical: aware-
ness/
reflect-
ion/
debate

ava
academia

Contents

Introduction

The Fundamentals of Interactive Design provides an introduction to the key principles of designing for interactive media. The presence of interactive media is increasing in every aspect of our lives from using a web browser to read about events, to buying music and playing video games (on consoles or on the Web). Digital interactive media is also social media (Twitter, Facebook, Google+); it's how we've begun to interact with each other and communicate. Interactive design is inherently non-passive, it is media that is delivered to an audience to be actively engaged with, played with, commented on, or sent on to others. It's a new approach to design, marketing and advertising, and it's a two-way conversation. The focus of this book is to take you step by step through each stage of the creative process – from inspiration to practical application of designing interfaces and interactive experiences. It provides an overview of the state of the art and the ongoing evolution of digital design, from where it is now to where it's going in the future.

The very nature of interactive hardware and software is always to change, update and improve. As such, it is difficult to get a firm handle on where interactive design is going. This book concentrates on those core elements and best practices required to create an 'agile designer', one who can adapt and change with new developments. Nothing in the design world is immune to changes in taste and technology, but as with all disciplines interactive design has principles that transcend the medium.

Design, at its core, is about communication, independent of the medium or media. Increasingly, interactive design's focus is on creating an experience through narratives and emotional connections. This approach is much the same in graphic design and fine arts, but interactive media allows for two-way communication and creates connections between brands, products and their audiences. How designers accomplish the goal of creating media that engages, entertains, communicates and 'sticks' with the audience is the focus of the first chapter of this book. In subsequent chapters, we examine some of the wider principles and media that are inherent to interactive design and are increasingly central to the world of marketing and advertising (can you think of any big companies who don't have a website or a Facebook/social media 'Like' button?). For the first time, a brand or company can communicate with their customers or fans (often via community managers who are employed to look after these relationships) in two-way conversations that build trust and brand loyalty.

Interactive media is everywhere, and designing for the multitude of web browsers, tablet devices and smart phones is the future of interactive design. However, it can become very technical if you don't focus on the key elements of why you're designing for that particular platform. The question is not 'How can I design for this new device or medium', but 'Why should I design for this platform or medium?' Deciding whether to jump onto the latest fad or technology bandwagon, just because it exists, can be a career-making or breaking decision for a designer (sadly, not all marketing departments follow this credo).

However, part of what it is to be an interactive designer is to experiment and push technologies into new and exciting areas. It's not until we play with interactive technologies that we begin to discover different uses or methods to communicate, often from unexpected places. With marketing and advertisers looking for new spaces and new touch points for their consumers, it's imperative that designers understand the interactive medium so that they are best able to use it to their advantage. Interactive designers need to make sure their designs are eye-catching, effective and engaging; they must be aware that other online distractions are never far away.

This book provides a solid grounding in the fundamentals of interactive communication and introduces best practices and case studies from industry experts in every chapter. These are important documentations of professional approaches to design briefs and are an invaluable tool to those new to the interactive design process.

The purpose of this book is not to be deeply technical about the minutiae of how to code or use software, but instead to give an overview of interactive technologies and design approaches within the medium, so you can begin to understand the process and nature of interactive design.

//start

KAISER CHIEFS
THE FUTURE IS MEDIEVAL

BACKGROUND   SIZE-O-METER   ROTATION

BACK

NEXT

1.1

Chapter 1: Interactive Design as a Discipline

1.1 **Kaiser Chiefs // Specialmoves and Wieden+Kennedy**

A detail from the Kaiser Chiefs' innovative album launch website
created by Specialmoves (UK) and Wieden+Kennedy (UK).
The project connected fans to the band by enabling them to
create their own version of the album and its artwork (see page 32).

What is interactive design?

Interactive design (also known as interactive media design or digital media design) covers a broad spectrum of media, including video games, educational DVDs, websites, mobile devices, television and touch-screen interfaces. This chapter introduces the interactive medium and the role of the interactive designer, and provides examples of engaging and experimental interactive-design projects.

Interaction as a medium

Interactive design expands and enriches traditional media; it allows audiences to engage, share, comment and interact with content, as opposed to static mediums (sometimes referred to as passive media, such as films, print and television) that require no direct interaction or feedback from its audience. Interactive design has become an important part of every medium, as brands and media companies want to connect with their consumers in more meaningful ways.

Interactive media is an enticing proposition for a number of reasons: it allows for updatable content and the inclusion of rich media (such as video), and enables interactions between consumers (for example, comments and conversations). Consumers are used to sharing content and have begun to expect more from their interactive experiences.

1.2–1.7 HBO Voyeur campaign // Big Spaceship

Big Spaceship (US) created an early online experiment for HBO. The *Voyeur* campaign invited the curious into the lives of fictional characters living in five different locations in New York City, using 12 videos and six audio tracks streaming throughout. The project won One Show Interactive gold and Cannes Lions gold.

'Learning never exhausts the mind.'

Leonardo da Vinci, artist and inventor

1.2

1.3

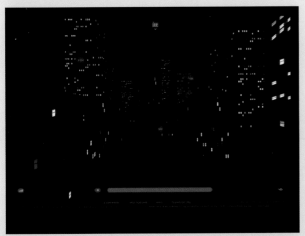

1.4

1.5

1.6

1.7

11

Design as a two-way conversation

Designing for any medium is about understanding the delivery elements of the medium and, importantly, the people who use it. There is a large focus on social media, but this is really an idea that dates back to the origins of the Web – it's about being able to share content between people. As soon as anyone could share anything electronically, they did; networks are designed specifically for that.

Once the new technology had become widely adopted and mainstream, forward-thinking brands and businesses began to investigate how they could get involved and started to develop strategies to take advantage of this new medium. This happened with every technological advance from print, to phones, television and digital media. What is new is the interactivity. For the first time, the conversation between brands and audiences is two way – people can share experiences and create their own content.

1.8 **Nike Air campaign //
Big Spaceship**

As early as 2006 big brands such as Nike were embracing interactive media. Big Spaceship, a Brooklyn-based digital creative **agency**, developed a Flash website for Nike's new Air Max line of running and basketball shoes. The aim was to translate the feeling of running directly on air into a digital experience.

1.8

1.9–1.13 **Nike Air campaign // Big Spaceship**

Users selected a runner or basketball player and then entered that person's world where, with simple keystrokes, they could trigger different animations and visual effects, and sample 'Life on Air'. The experience combined animation, photography, green-screen video, original sound and interactive design.

1.9

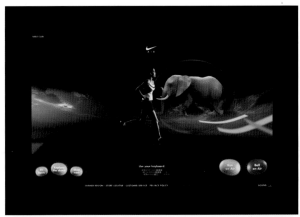

1.10

1.11

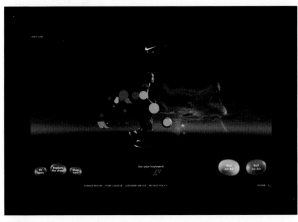

1.12

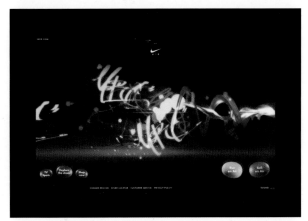

1.13

User-generated content (UGC)

Interactive technologies enable people worldwide to create, exchange and share content. This could be in the form of text, videos, music or pictures. This is called 'user-generated content' and examples include the videos that you see on YouTube and the non-commercial material you find on Facebook (beyond the interface and layout). It's a powerful new addition to the media world and companies such as Facebook, Twitter and YouTube have sprung up around it.

Engineers and interactive designers have developed these new technologies and expanded them into areas no one could have imagined even ten years ago.

1.14–1.20 Lips // AKQA

AKQA's (US) *Xbox Lips* (a video game singing experience) jukebox campaign linked users' Facebook images to a karaoke game that overlaid animated lips synced to an audio track. Merging **user-generated content** with social media, the lips campaign leveraged social media and user-generated content in an engaging way. The interface and interactions had to be simple and immediate for the project to work well, and the videos produced by users could then be shared.

1.14

1.15

1.16

1.17

1.18

1.19

1.20

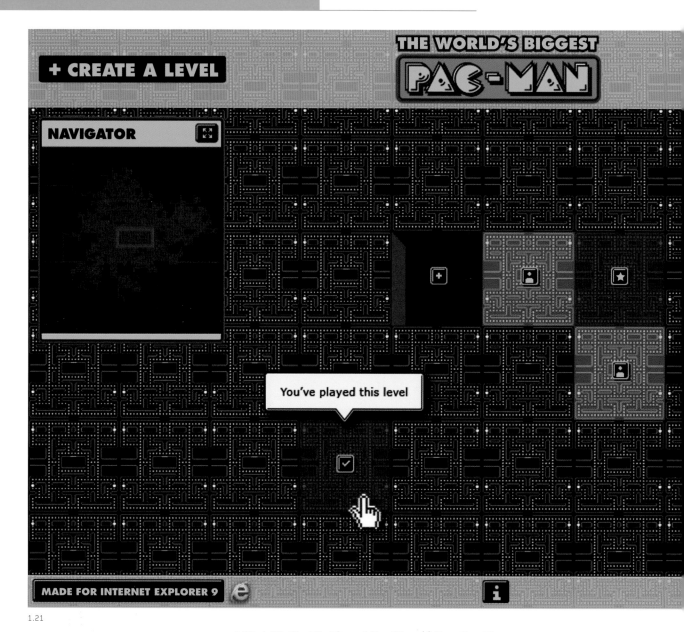

1.21

1.21–1.26 World's Biggest Pac-Man // Soap Creative

This website asked visitors to create their own Pac-Man maze and connect them using Facebook. Every user-created maze is connected and can be explored when logged into the Facebook part of the campaign. Using HTML5 visitors can use the iconic Pac-Man gameplay as a basis for their own user-created maze. The site was created as part of a campaign for Microsoft's Internet Explorer 9. The site also logged user and country statistics with a global tally of game data that grew along with the site.

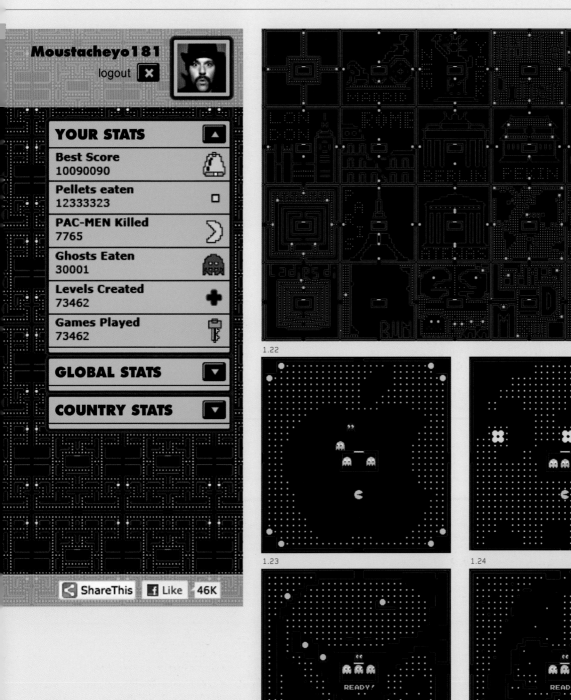

Moustacheyo181
logout ✖

YOUR STATS ▲

Best Score
10090090

Pellets eaten
12333323

PAC-MEN Killed
7765

Ghosts Eaten
30001

Levels Created
73462

Games Played
73462

GLOBAL STATS ▼

COUNTRY STATS ▼

ShareThis   f Like 46K

1.22

1.23

1.24

READY!

READY!

1.25

1.26

1.27

1.28

1.29

1.30

1.31

1.27–1.31 Most Awesomest Thing Ever // Big Spaceship

Big Spaceship created a project called *Most Awesomest Thing Ever* as a fun experiment in user-created content. The website initially pulled a list of odd combinations from Wikipedia, such as ninjas, naps and Mount Everest, and asked users to vote on which was 'most awesome'. As the project took off, users could upload their own images to battle against other things, and this has extended the life of the project.

Interaction teams

Interactive design has secured a place in the global design field very quickly. In order to address the demand for interactive content more and more design agencies and studios are creating in-house interaction teams (as opposed to outsourcing or using freelance designers). Some traditional graphic design studios have completely switched their focus towards digital interaction. Internationally renowned design studios Big Spaceship, AKQA and IDEO are amongst the largest interactive/digital success stories of recent years because they embraced interactive design completely. New delivery methods and communication strategies are enabling the discipline to take its place at the forefront of the design industry. So what skills and mindset are required to become an interactive designer?

1.32–1.34 Contradictions //
Big Spaceship

In 2011, Big Spaceship launched *The Contradictions Project* for Starburst. The project sought to encourage fans to celebrate human contradictions and help fund music education programmes across the country. Elements included a Flash Facebook application that allowed people to submit their own contradictions, iPad and touch-screen installations, and Times Square JumboTron updates.

Starburst, It's a Juicy Contradiction and all affiliated designs are trademarks of the Wm. Wrigley Jr. Company or its subsidiaries.

1.32

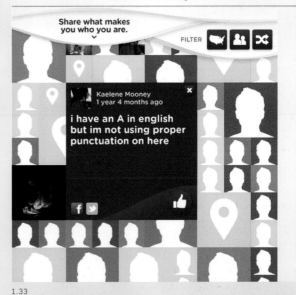

1.33

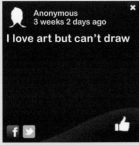

1.34

What does an interactive designer do?

Interactive design is a constantly evolving medium. It's a career choice that continually excites and challenges both new and experienced designers to draw on multiple skill sets to produce engaging work. The emphasis is always on the experience the audience is having with the project and the relationship being built between the consumer and the content producer.

Designing engagement

All visual communication is about impact, audience engagement and the communication of a message. Interactive designers will experiment and innovate by using different technologies to engage the audience in new ways. The focus is on creating positive experiences for the intended consumer. This is fairly straightforward in traditional media, such as television or print. However, in interactive design the medium crosses many creative boundaries, from product design (the interfaces on MP3 players or TVs) to the Web, gaming, mobiles and tablets. All of these media operate in different spaces that need to be considered.

Whether creating a product for a single platform or multiple platforms, designers still have to address the experience that the audience will have and how it will differ from competitors. The design team will have to ask themselves: what is the difference between a mobile experience and a television experience? Is one experience richer than the other or are they just different? Where do people use interactive media?' An interactive media designer uses multiple experimental and cognitive skills to create a deep and engaging experience for a client's intended audience. (**User experience design** – also known as UX design – is covered in detail in chapter 2.)

1.35

1.35–1.43 Smirnoff // Specialmoves

Interactive touch screens placed in airports connected travellers to Smirnoff's *Nightlife Exchange Project*. By selecting a destination, users could tap into the content produced by the Nightlife Exchange at some of the world's most iconic party locations.

The project worked on different levels dependent on the amount of time the traveller had. A cursory interaction might just show a concert video or party information. More time spent with the project enabled the user to have access to more content and a deeper engagement with the brand.

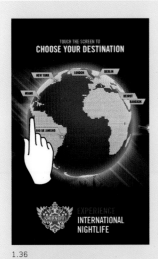

1.36

1.37

1.38

1.39

1.40

1.41

1.42

1.43

21

1.44

1.45

1.46

1.47

1.48

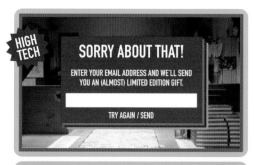

1.49

Concentration and passions

In interactive design it's imperative that designers keep up with advances in their discipline. A passion for technology and innovation, along with forward-thinking, imagination and the ability to generate great ideas are what make a successful interactive designer.

Universities and colleges offer a wide variety of courses within the interactive media field and students on these courses are encouraged to build a portfolio that best reflects their passions and abilities – this could be in game design (creating games that engage, educate or entertain), **interface design** (for mobile devices, the Web or products), **physical computing** (using sensors, motors and computers to create an interactive sculpture or **animatronics**) or it could be in application design (for example, Android apps and iPhone apps).

Teamwork

Having passion and a solid skill set is good, but design is a collaborative process. Although interactive designers must be aware of the many aspects of their medium, no one designer is expected to know everything. To be able to create an innovative or engaging solution to a design problem, designers work in **teams**. Many voices are required to launch a great project, so it is crucial that interactive designers are able to work well with others. When creating a design solution, it's the ability to conceptualize and present ideas coherently and passionately that is important. Once a team has a direction and a design solution is agreed on, additional project members are brought in for particular tasks, and to achieve specific goals (e.g. artists, coders, animators and interface designers). The interactive designer has to be able to work with these groups to realize the vision of the project.

1.44–1.50
Hans Brinker Budget Hotel // KesselsKramer

The Hans Brinker Budget Hotel in Amsterdam is famous for its advertisement as the 'Worst hotel in the world'. As part of a campaign, KesselsKramer (Netherlands) created an interactive virtual receptionist who seems to react live to users' requests for help. This playful, humorous site dares users to interact with the grumpy receptionist and the outcome is often quite negative (but funny). This project fits well with the wider brand identity by creating an engaging experience that has multiple combinations of questions with multiple responses.

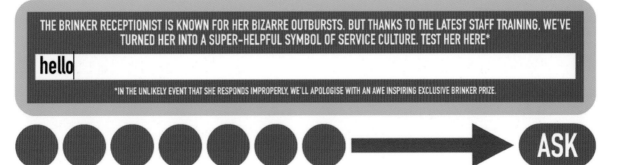

1.50

23

Interview: Darrell Wilkins, creative director

Darrell Wilkins has worked in the interactive design industry for more than 18 years, and was co-founder of Specialmoves. He has seen many changes within the interactive medium: from no one understanding what it was, to the burst of the dot com bubble and finally, the acceptance of the medium in the design industry.

What is an interactive designer?

Interactive designers are often people frustrated with the world around them, but rather than complain, they think up ways to make it better. Most people are reasonable problem solvers, but people who really understand the problems are usually good at interactive design.

Clearly interaction isn't just about digital; people design all sorts of things. The challenge for any interactive designer is the same. How can you create something so that people understand how to use it without thinking hard about it?

What does a studio look for in an interactive designer?

When interviewing people, I ask them about ticket machines, bathroom taps/faucets, doors and service station car park signs. The responses illustrate their understanding of how people actually interact with everyday objects and information.

I want to know if they have thought about interactivity outside of the confines of the Web or monitor, and how they relate to everyday interactions.

I also ask 'oddball' questions to see how designers think on their feet. There is no wrong or right answer, I just want to know how the designer thinks and, if possible, what quirky or unusual responses I might get. These are methods of finding out more about the 'real' designer and how he or she approaches design – if the designer lives and breathes it, or just thinks of it as a job.

What do you feel is the future for the interactive design industry?

I believe the future of the industry lies in a significant shift towards brilliantly designed interactivity that positively affects people's lives. The studios, brands and services that succeed will be those that make people happier, more productive and help solve their problems. At its heart, the question is always: how do I make this a better experience, and for what purpose?

1.51–1.53 Lynx // Specialmoves

Not all work for clients is 'front end' videos and content. Sometimes a client will seek expertise in the delivery of existing content. In this case, Lynx were looking for a content management system (CMS) solution that would allow them to deliver a variety of media and content in multiple languages. The CMS is a dynamic platform onto which the client can load pre-created web content that is then accessible to customers.

1.51

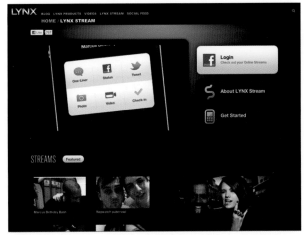

1.52

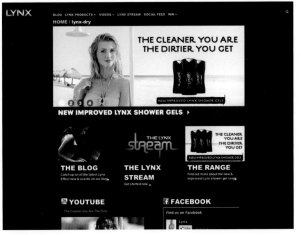

1.53

The design document

Documentation of the design process is very important; in fact, it's mandatory for most companies. The design document expresses the vision for the project, describes its contents and the plans for implementation.

A good design document expresses the project in enough detail that it can be given to any team member or outside party (contract programmers for example) and they would be able to work on the project from the specifications given. There are usually two copies, one for the studio development team and one for the client. The studio version is more technical and can be shared with other teams or contractors. The client version is less technical and more of a map of the process from beginning to end.

All design documents are different but should generally include these subject areas:

1   Table of contents and an introduction: these describe the purpose of the project, scope, document organization, the audience, and terms and definitions.

2   A design overview: the project approach, goals and constraints, and the project's guiding principles.

3   The design specifications: colours to be used, palettes, images, overall aesthetic and feeling.

4   Wireframes: the initial design prototypes, sketches, **personas and scenarios**.

5   Project architecture: the technical aspects of the project, the requirements for programming, hardware and software and how the project will be launched.

6   The implementation plan: this sets out project management requirements, time frames, costings and budgets.

7   Rules: these are the client-specific constraints (use of colours, logos and client-specific language).

8   Testing and **usability**: the plan of what is going to be tested, how the prototypes will be tested, and what **metrics** and measurements are to be used.

9   Assumptions and studio constraints: general values and implications of using a target audience. For example, if the project is a website there would be an assumption that the client's audience knows at least how to access a website and use a browser's navigation system.

These subject areas are some of the elements that go into a design document. Only those parts of the document that connected directly to the designer would be written by him/her. The overall job of collating the larger document is usually the job of the project manager. However, it is an important part of a designer's education to learn how to write a document and to be able to use it to communicate ideas clearly.

1.54–1.57 Design document // Caius Eugene

This image is an example of a student design document for a final project. It goes into detail about the research, production and process of creating the project (a video game in this case). It's not as detailed as a professional design document, but it does show many of the subject areas.

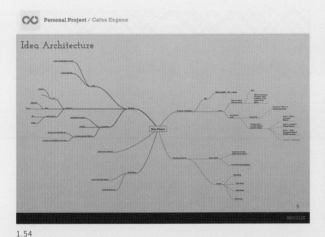

1.54

1.55

1.56

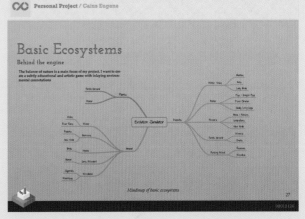

1.57

27

Using new technology

The technology that interactive designers use is continually developing. Designers must keep up to date with new innovations and choose those that will help to enhance their interactive projects. As a junior designer or student starting out, you will find that there are technologies in ascendency and ones that few people know about, but which may be useful in creating new and fascinating design solutions.

Make it remixable

Projects such as the *The Symphony* for Louis Vuitton (see opposite) and the launch of the new Kaiser Chiefs' album (see page 32) are good examples of the customizable and remixable culture of the future. Interactivity is not a one-way medium – consumers expect to be able to view or interact with content, comment on it and share it with others immediately. And to do so wherever they are connected, from home computers to mobile phones and tablets. Enabling an audience to change or play with the content being provided leads to a deeper engagement; it's no longer a project people just look at or click on, it's something that they have a creative stake in.

Remixing may not work for every project, but if people are willing to spend their own time using assets or content from a project and then share them, the design team knows that they have something special; the project can become a phenomenon and expand far beyond its original intended audience.

1.58–1.61 The Symphony // Kokokaka

Kokokaka (Sweden) collaborated with Louis Vuitton to create a playful interactive musical experience as part of the campaign for the fashion house's Small Leather Goods range. The project allows users to explore and play with the merchandise whilst creating a custom soundtrack or 'symphony'. The interaction connects the customer to the designer's range in a quirky and unusual way. It's generated on the fly and creates a unique audio experience each visit. The soundtrack is created by 'drawing' over the products (see image 1.58), effectively using the items as notes or keys to create a melody.

1.58

1.59

1.60

1.61

Make it mobile

The mobile platform is developing quickly. Mobile usually refers to smartphones and tablets rather than laptop computers. Arguably, the first smartphone arrived in 2001 with the advent of the Microsoft Windows CE operating system. These devices have come a long way with the introduction of brighter screens and faster connectivity. With the increase in 3G or 4G networks, the possibilities for interactive media on these devices have exploded. People can connect from almost anywhere and this ultimately changes how media and products are consumed.

Interactive designers must be comfortable designing for both large-screen monitors and small screens on tablets or OLED phones (this is known as **responsive design**). Developing an app can be all that is needed for a project, or it could be part of a campaign that includes other media platforms such as the Web. Mobile adds an interesting element – by using GPS (global positioning systems), apps can locate people, and people can share where they are immediately, along with any content in their surroundings. App stores for the main platforms Android and Apple iOS are increasing in content every day; designers have to decide if a certain platform is right for their project and if it is, develop an engaging solution for that platform.

1.62–1.64
Heineken app // AKQA

AKQA developed an iPhone app for Heineken with the UEFA Champion's League. A player can predict team scores within a short deadline to win points. Each point can be shared with friends via the app or Facebook. The app connects to the live football match, supplying statistics, quizzes and scores in real-time, extending the reach of the brands beyond just the football competition.

1.63

1.64

1.65

1.66

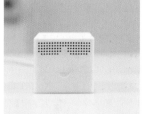

1.67

Design different

Computers are being embedded into all kinds of products; this is sometimes referred to as '**ubiquitous computing**', meaning that computers are everywhere. For example, computers in cars help mechanics to diagnose problems, and fridges monitor their own contents and create shopping lists for their owners. The common factor in all of these **smart devices** is that they all need to talk to each other and to people, creating what is known as 'The Internet of Things'. Soon, many devices will be interconnected and swapping information. The trick is to find ways of developing projects that exploit these devices in interesting ways.

One way is to look at new technology and see if it has other, originally unintended uses to exploit. Two recent examples are the Nintendo Wii remote hacks and Microsoft Kinect hacks. These devices were designed to complement or control video-game consoles, but as with much technology people wanted to repurpose it. Drivers for the Kinect device were made available as **open source** online (Microsoft supported this) and quickly people were using this sophisticated 3D-tracking hardware for other uses, none of them game related but all of them interesting.

The Wii Remote uses Bluetooth to talk to the Wii hardware and consequently, software quickly appeared online, and the Wii Remotes that were used had nothing to do with Nintendo's original application. (For more information see <kinecthacks.com> and <hackawii.com/category/wiimote-hack>.)

The ability to see possibilities beyond what software or hardware is designed for is an essential part of interactive design. Clients may think they need a new website, but perhaps what they really need is interactive sports shoes in key stores that enable customers to share their experiences via social media. It's curiosity that drives innovation and change, creating ever more engaging and entertaining products or experiences.

1.65–1.67 **Polly and Olly // Mint Digital**

Mint Digital (UK) created two USB-enabled experimental devices that react with their owners' social networks. Polly (image 1.66) delivers a sweet to her owner as a reward for retweeting. Olly (image 1.67) rewards his owner with a fragrance every time they are mentioned on Twitter. These devices connect the social media space with the environment of the user in a fun and playful way.

Case study: Kaiser Chiefs' website

Studio: Specialmoves, UK
Client: Kaiser Chiefs **Advertising agency:** Wieden+Kennedy

Specialmoves were tasked with building a launch 'event' website for the UK band Kaiser Chiefs' new album. They created a space that enabled fans to customize and share new music and artwork.

Kaiser Chiefs' interactive album

Kaiser Chiefs are an indie band from the north of England. When they wanted to launch their fourth album, *The Future is Medieval*, they defined a design problem for their advertising agency Wieden+Kennedy: how do we create something different that will be engaging for current fans, but will also create media buzz, to attract new fans to the band?

The interactive design studio Specialmoves won the contract and worked with Wieden+Kennedy to come up with an answer: create an innovative album-launch website, as only interactive media can, and use it to deliver an exciting experience to fans, new and old.

From concept to prototype

The idea for the website <kaiserchiefs.com> was to introduce the audience to a series of 'machines' that users could interact with to create their own album version. When fans accessed the website, they could pick ten tracks out of a possible 20, in any order they liked. They could then use an interface to create custom artwork for their album, then buy it. The fans have created their own version of the Kaiser Chiefs' album complete with custom artwork.

Thinking further, having persuaded fans to create their own versions, the site would allow the fans to sell their customized albums to other fans. To sweeten the deal, they would receive £1 ($1.60 USD) for every copy of their custom album that they sold. So the fans could actually make money out of the Kaiser Chiefs' album! It was an interesting solution to the design **brief** and the band loved the idea.

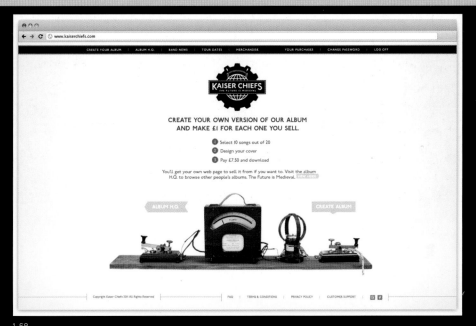

1.68

1.68 **Launch website // Specialmoves**

In 2011 Specialmoves and Wieden+Kennedy created a bespoke album creation experience for UK band Kaiser Chiefs. The digital platform placed the fans at the heart of the album release giving them the tools to create and sell their own version of the album.

1.69 **Album generator // Specialmoves**

Kaiser Chiefs recorded 20 songs, fans could choose ten of them and customize their artwork. The fans could use a bespoke web page to promote their new album.

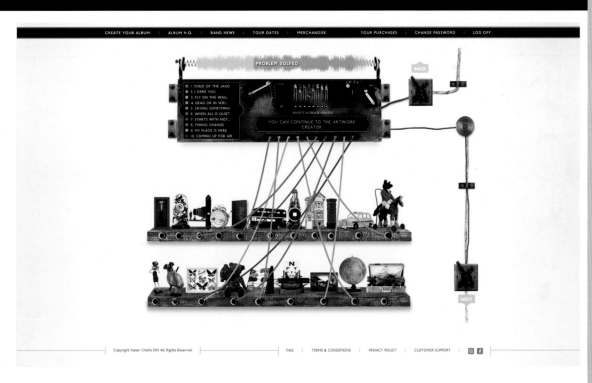

1.69

1.70

1.71

1.70–1.71 Fans created cover designs // Specialmoves

Fans paid £7.50 and for every sale they received £1. This use of fan engagement and social promotion broke with the conventional model of releasing an album.

The prototype phase

With a limited budget, the team decided that the most important thing to do would be to concentrate on the album generation and payment areas first; they could use this as a base because if they couldn't figure out that part of the core idea, the entire concept would fall apart.

The first job was to research the payment side of the idea; it was felt that if fans weren't encouraged by receiving a small payback, they may not bother to create custom albums, which was the main feature of the site. The team worked on creating a proof of concept (a rough draft that works just enough to validate the process). By using this, they would know when someone bought a fan's album so both the record label and the album creator would get their money. Once this was done, the team moved on to the creating and sharing aspect of the project.

The team's back-end developers created a working prototype, which took ten MP3 files selected by a user, copied them to a folder and embedded an image into that folder. It then archived those files into a format for easy download.

At this point, it seemed that the website's main goal (payments to fans, album buying and remixed album sharing) seemed achievable. The issue now was speed. In an age of iTunes and instant gratification, people are used to getting their music in a matter of seconds. It's one thing to have one fan create-download-and-sell, but what happens when 400 or 700 people want to use the service all at the same time? The client doesn't want to see crashed websites or fans having to wait for minutes with an hourglass spinning in front of them. This is where the **front-end designers** sat down with the **back-end developers** and thrashed out solutions and compromises that would work and work well. It's rare to have to compromise on the overall aesthetic, it's usually the constraints of the hardware or technology that raises issues. At this point, communication between programmers and interactive designers is crucial – everyone has to be on the same page, one miscommunication and the project could go awry.

Communication and compromise

The team knew from experience that if what they needed to achieve couldn't work one way there may be a solution that would deliver a similar outcome. Sometimes the team will have to alter the idea to accommodate technological shortcomings, so the better the team is at presenting and explaining their ideas and the project to the development team, the easier it is to achieve results everyone is happy with. Communication is always the key to achieving the aims of the project.

In the process of meeting with the back-end developers one technical issue that came up was that the team had no idea how many albums they would need to deliver. The best part about this project was that no one had really done this before; this was also the most worrying and challenging part of the process. This is where prototyping becomes such an essential part of the process of design. Creating small, easily broken prototypes means that they can be tested, rebuilt and improved. Each failure in the process means the next prototype will be stronger.

Therefore, the practice is to iterate constantly and quickly towards the end product. Once the prototypes began to work, the team was able to build a rough working draft of the project that could be shown to the client to get them excited and raise their expectations of what the project would be like.

Working with client expectations

Once a robust prototype was ready, it was shown to the client. The idea was to get the client excited about the team's solution so that they could start their own marketing and PR engines when the site launched. Kaiser Chiefs' site was going to be innovative, technically challenging and would hopefully receive of lot of attention from fans and the media. All of this had to be sold to the client by the project management team.

Whilst the initial scope was simply defined in a set of **user stories** (storyboards), it became apparent that the client needed to know up front and in detail how core features were going to work. It's all very well simply proposing a concept but a client wants to know if it's feasible and deliverable. Along with the early prototype, the team also produced a series of materials that enabled the planning and smooth execution of the website, such as a **wireframe** of the site. Wireframes are used by interactive designers to outline the entire website, the navigation, layout and content formats. It's a form of early prototyping that allows the team and the client to discuss colour choices, navigation issues and any areas of importance or focus on any individual page. As such, wireframes are essential tools for communicating the early development of a site to everyone involved in the project.

'You need to let a user know what you're doing and what they need to do in a few short, snappy sentences. In this respect, summing up what the Kaiser Chiefs' site does is pretty simple.'

Darrell Wilkins, creative director, Specialmoves

Collaboration

When a studio is working in small teams, such as at Specialmoves, it's a collaborative undertaking between the design team and the client. At first, the team is closely connected to the client, then the team will go off and prototype and, as the project begins to take shape, return for more meetings.

All the while, the project is tweaked, changed, managed and evolves. As the client sees the working prototypes, they can step back and leave the team to develop the concept fully, knowing that the team is capable of delivering the final project. These small but important growth spurts and constant communication of ideas and prototypes are crucial for everyone involved when working to a deadline. Everyone has to be on the same page and must have full knowledge of what is required of them. This collaborative process creates a stronger project as the client has input and may suggest changes, along with every creative team member. Once the goals and expectations are set, the project can be finalized and delivered.

1.72

1.72–1.74 Promotional assets

Fans received a suite of banners and a PDF poster based on their artwork to promote their album. The site tracked best-selling versions, individual sales and social media interactions.

1.73

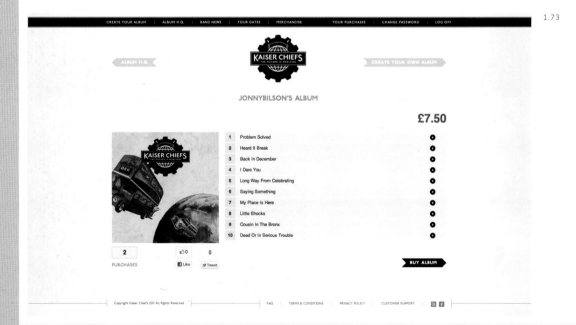

1.74

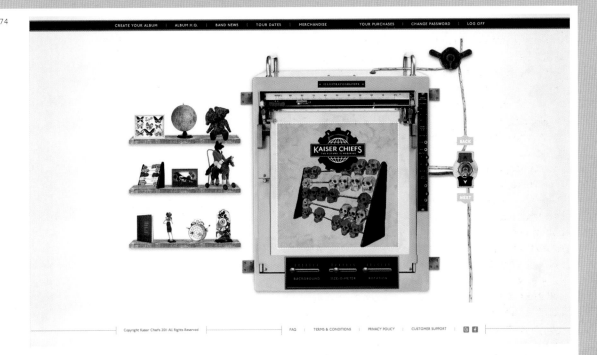

The end result

The launched website is a product that has taken many people and many different skill sets to produce. The process of assembling a team, producing concepts, undergoing research, sketching, wireframing and then prototyping, is a typical interactive design approach to an innovative project. When the website went live in 2011 the press loved it, and many users ended up buying two albums each to get the full set of 20 tracks (which was great for the band and for the record company!). The site has gone on to garner media attention and win awards, but the best feedback is from the fans of the band, 'Mind. Blown.'

PROJECT TOOLS

- Adobe Flash (CS4)
- Adobe Photoshop (CS4)
- ELMAH (logging)
- Microsoft .NET MVC.
- Taglib-Sharp (for ID3 tagging)
- Ionic.Zip (for archiving/zipping)
- Autofac (dependency injector)
- Squish It (css/javascript squisher)
- Google Analytics
- Robotlegs
- BulkLoader
- Greensock TweenMax
- HTML
- jQuery

Project: Create concepts and storyboards

The brief

Create a concept website (include layouts, art assets, navigation and interface) for a band as part of their new album launch. Devise and create an innovative engagement mechanism or marketing hook that will encourage visitors to the site. The site should work for existing fans as well as new fans.

Remember that designing experiences for audiences is the mainstay of the interactive designer. Telling stories and enabling audiences to create their own meaning is an integral part of the design process. This project offers you the chance to practise this process and develop your skills as they would be applied in industry.

1 Research

Produce a sketch outline of your ideas for the launch based on your research into the band and other artists' launch campaigns. Compile the research into a document that you can refer back to for inspiration and direction.

Consideration

■ Research other band websites and their launches. Research your chosen band's aesthetic and their music and feed that into the art-asset generation for the website.

2 Moodboard

Create a moodboard of visuals, colours and inspirations for the project.
A moodboard should represent the emotional context portrayed in the project;
it becomes a visual guide to the emotional feel that will be used in the images,
layouts and art assets. Use the moodboard as a springboard for creating art assets
for the prototype. The site should have at least four content areas, for example
discography, store, tour dates and 'about the band'.

3 Interactive storyboard

Create an interactive design storyboard (i.e. a mock-up) of the site. This could
be created in PowerPoint or Keynote, in an HTML editor or other media-creation
software. It should be a prototype of the interactive elements of the site (buttons
that are clicked that go to other content areas, videos or animations can be
embedded). The mock-up should focus on explaining the innovative solution to the
design problem. The innovation may be very technical or very simple depending on
the idea. The site prototype will consist of the following components:

(a)   A navigation interface.

(b)   At least four content areas with art assets and multimedia
(video, music, images).

(c)   The 'innovative' fan engagement mechanism (e.g. treasure hunts, remixing,
competitions, social media or video games). This part may need several slides/
pages/areas to communicate the concept in sufficient depth.

Considerations

- The site might exist across mobile technologies or in an app.

- The site could involve setting up live chats/social-media feeds between fans
and the band. How could or should social media be included?

- Could remixing be involved? Perhaps of the band video or tracks? Fans could
create their own versions based on tracks from the new album.

- What happens after the initial album launch? Is there anything in the site that
would keep users coming back over a longer period?

Tips!

1   Spend time on
the research.
2   Don't spend
too long on a
moodboard.
3   Storyboards must
be compelling.
4   Don't use 'magic'
– be realistic.

2.1

Chapter 2:
Ideas, Prototypes and Experiences

2.1 IKEA Soffar // Kokokaka

This is an HTML5-based interactive video project created by Kokokaka (Sweden) for Forsman & Bodenfors (F&B) for their client IKEA. It connected an offline media campaign with the online by producing an interactive video experience using assets taken from TV broadcast adverts, along with images from the print campaign (more on pages 52–53).

Where do ideas come from?

'Everyday people are not very good designers.'

Donald Norman, user-centred design expert

Many young designers ask: where do all these great ideas come from? How does an interactive designer progress from an outline in a brief to a final engaging project? As with any creative endeavour it breaks down into several parts: research, inspiration and perspiration. A good designer can be creative based on research and hard work; an excellent designer relies on all three elements.

Inspiration

Inspiration is an often over used word, but ultimately it's about trusting instincts, often gained from a combination of experience and leaps of faith. Belief and passion for design is important, as is being open to new ideas. Designers need to be able to translate those ideas into tangible digital artefacts and interactions. To facilitate inspirational moments designers may, like artists and musicians, surround themselves with objects that inspire them, for example, design books, magazines, products and whimsical items.

2.2

2.2–2.7 Creative labs // IDEO

Many design studios have 'labs' or in-house experimental diffusers of concepts and prototypes. The developments may never be used in commercial work, but the process of 'just to find out' is critical for innovative studios. Shown opposite are images from a number of such activities held recently in IDEO's offices globally, including 'Hack Nights' and 'Make-a-Thons'. IDEO is a leading design and innovation firm and these activities promote creativity and experimentation.

2.3

2.6

2.4

2.5

2.7

Influences and the creative process

'The ultimate inspiration is the deadline.'

Nolan Bushnell, founder of Atari

Designers sometimes hit a creative brick wall. There is a point while looking at a straightforward brief when the client may add the crucial question, 'Can the team produce something fresh?' The client needs a project that is different in order to maximize marketplace impact and build that all-important media buzz.

Research the design problem

The first step in creating an inspired solution to a brief comes from stepping back and defining the design problem succinctly. If the design team don't understand the problem the brief is asking them to answer, the team will not be able to create a solution. In short: define the problem then solve that problem. This is where research is such a crucial weapon in the designer's arsenal. Exploring the client's business, who they are and how they have executed ideas before, are all background essentials. The other side is to look at the competition: who are they and what are they doing? Research and query is the first step in idea generation.

'Good design is a lot like clear thinking made visual.'

Edward Tufte, data visualization pioneer

2.8 Converse // IDEO

IDEO, a leading design and innovation firm, helped iconic shoemakers Converse create a brand strategy and service model that would appeal to its legions of devotees. When developing the first stand-alone store, the team at IDEO started thinking about the atmosphere of the space rather than the look.

By talking with Converse loyalists, the team developed an aesthetic to celebrate the core brand message – self-expression. One approach was an interactive space and interface in which customers could be creative. Custom shoe-making stations allowed shoppers to design their own one-of-a-kind pair of shoes using Converse's shoe-printing technology.

IDEO/Coutler Lewis

2.8

Be creative all the time

Many designers are motivated by starting to work on a project. The creativity comes through the process of doodling, drawing, sketching and playing. For others, inspiration comes from being deeply embedded in popular culture, technology, art and history. Inspiration for tackling a design problem really has to come from engaging with it head on.

2.9

2.10

2.9–2.11
Finding inspiration

Inspiration for aesthetics and visuals are all around every designer – from street graffiti to signs, books, artwork and galleries. Designers are always students, learning every day and adding to the culture surrounding them. Designers of any discipline need to keep a detailed visual sketchbook that documents environments, emotions, narratives and themes. It will serve as a repository for inspiration at any time.

Denise Jacobs from alistapart.com created a five-point guide to getting inspired:

1 'Gamify' your work: be playful when approaching a problem. Adopting a play-based approach to problem solving creates a more open mindset that is less stressed and more open to inspiration.

2 Commit to overcome self-chosen challenges: if a project's technical requirements seem hard to accomplish, spin that as a positive and use it as an opportunity to grow as a designer.

3 Set clear goals and actionable steps: break down any large overwhelming process into smaller chunks that are more manageable. Create a reward system for when each challenge has been met (for example, once a task is completed, take a break or go for a walk) and this can become a great motivator.

4 Keep upping the ante: always remain optimistic and view each 'failure' in a project as a step towards the larger goal of creating that totally amazing end product. Focus on every positive achievement as this adds to confidence levels and satisfaction in the job.

5 Make it epic: think of the struggle for inspiration as a personal 'heroic' struggle towards an end goal. Become excited about how the project could change lives or create a buzz amongst your peers.

Making the process of design into an internalized game is a good way to get creativity flowing. The other approach is to simply talk to others. Talking about the problem is a way of engaging with it and solutions will start to present themselves because of that engagement.

Brainstorming, sketching and idea generation

Designers may use several techniques to start the creative process. One is a method called **brainstorming**; it's a group creativity technique and should be as spontaneous as possible. Usually, a word or the design problem will be the starting point; from there the team will throw words or associated ideas around to try to conceptualize multiple meanings or to create a different 'out-there' approach to the problem. Brainstorming is sometimes referred to as 'blue-sky thinking'. Designers could start with a focus from the client's brief such as 'fun, engaging, youth oriented' and end up with associations, themes, images and definitions of what that statement represents. Brainstorming is used to get out of thinking of the obvious and allows a team to develop different approaches to design problems.

Once the brainstorming session has exhausted all possibilities, the next step is to clarify the ideas so that they work within the confines of time and budgets. A tangible or popular concept is then taken on-board by the development team to begin production on sketching a prototype.

'We are the most innovative when we collaborate.'

Samuel J. Palmisano, Chairman of IBM

2.11

Sketching and wireframing

Sketching is visual thinking; you don't have to be a great artist or illustrator to be able to communicate or develop an idea using sketches. Industries and products can begin with a 'sketch on the back of a napkin' and so it is with generating ideas. Sketching formulates the essence of a project and begins the process of moving towards the end goal.

Wireframing works in a similar way to sketching. For interactive designers a wireframe is a sketch that outlines a project's interactive components. For example, for a website this could be navigation and layout. Wireframes are useful for quickly establishing a project's requirements before any coding or asset creation begins.

In his article, 'Sketching: the Visual Thinking Power Tool', Mike Rohde explains that because sketches are rough and unfinished they actually invite more discussion. A sketch is an incomplete idea and so no one is going to get offended if there is any critique of the sketch because no significant effort has been put into it. Sketches are also disposable, which invites more honest discussion and iteration of ideas.

2.12

**2.12–2.13 Heartland website redesign //
Mike Rohde and Brian Artka, Northwoods Software
Development**

Sketches allow clients and designers to discuss elements of the design before it has been fixed. They are rough to allow for flexibility and not visual enough to lock in any aesthetics.

This website redesign for Heartland Funds, a Milwaukee-based (US) mutual fund firm started as a simple wireframe (see image 2.13). The sketch maintains an indicative visual that does not fix the client into colour schemes and rich imagery. As Mike Rohde explains 'I made pencil sketches on grid paper for the wireframes, to capture my ideas for the structure, with notes on the margins to provide details for the client'.

Reprinted with the permission of Mike Rohde (rohdesign.com) / *A List Apart* magazine (alistapart.com) and the author[s].

'Sketching is great for rapid idea generation.'

Mike Rohde, designer and writer

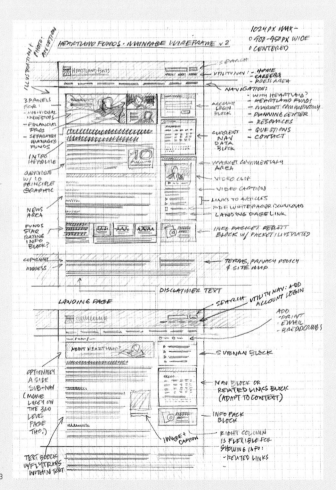

2.13

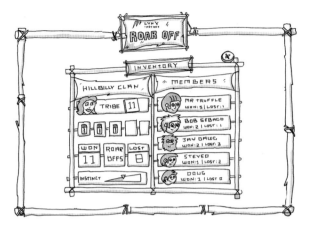

2.14

2.15

2.16

2.17

2.18

2.19

2.20

2.14–2.20 Lynx Instinct campaign // Soap Creative

As a project develops so do the sketches and wireframes. In these examples, the wireframes created by Soap Creative (Australia) are well realized with most of the content used in the final Instinct campaign for Lynx. Even at this stage the team can tweak the interface, change layouts and colour schemes before finalizing the design. Images 2.18–20 show the final realization of the campaign and in-game advertising content for the *Ghost Recon 2* video game (the campaign also ran in several other titles).

The medium informs the design

'If your user interface even vaguely resembles an airplane cockpit, you're doing it wrong.'

John Gruber, creator of Daring Fireball blog

Once ideas and concepts have been sketched out and a direction for the project has emerged, the technical design process can begin. As discussed in chapter 1, understanding the medium of interactive design is important, but also, the medium should never restrict an idea or experience because the limits can always be pushed. A compromise between a concept's execution and what's deliverable is usually reached with the first prototype.

2.21–2.28
Fiat eco:Drive // AKQA

AKQA developed an engaging animated desktop application for Fiat's eco:Drive technology. The application analyses data collected from the car and delivers eco:Drive information in an aesthetically quirky, easy-to-understand format.

The desktop application delivers rich data that could be confusing to many users. The challenge for the AKQA developers was to communicate dry statistical data in an entertaining and accessible way.

The prototype
An idea can become a viable prototype if members of the design team understand the delivery space in which they are working. To understand the medium, designers have to create a technical prototype. This is often referred to as **proof of concept**, and allows the technical team members to demonstrate that the idea will work. While the technology is being decided, other team members are working on aspects such as art and interface assets. The technical proof of concept proves the viability of the project; the next step is to answer the question: how will people actually experience this product?

2.21

2.22

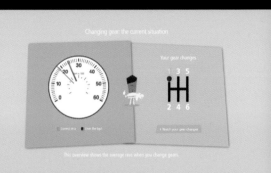

2.23

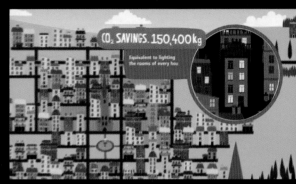

2.24

2.25

2.26

2.27

2.28

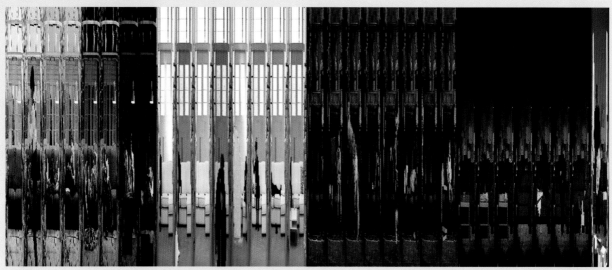

2.29

2.30

2.31

2.29–2.36 IKEA Soffar // Kokokaka

Kokokaka created this website for Forsman & Bodenfors (F&B) and their client IKEA using HTML5. The challenge was to combine images from a print campaign with video from the TV commercials, and then seamlessly sync the images with quirky music. As users play with the interface to access different stills and videos, the music beats in synch with the on-screen action. The developers used HTML5 because there is far less lag, even with large video files, as the browser doesn't have to load plug-ins such as QuickTime or Flash.

2.32

2.33

2.34

2.35

2.36

Emotional attachment to the product

In many ways, the experience is the most important aspect of any design, it's the process of thinking through and answering the question: what is the audience getting out of this? If people feel that they have had a rewarding or entertaining experience, then they will associate positive feelings with the product or brand.

Creating emotional contact and connection

Emotions attached to experiences are very important. For example, the emotional state filmgoers are in when coming out of a great movie may compel them to purchase extra merchandise or see the movie again; it will certainly mean that they will share their thoughts on the movie with others. It works in reverse as well – people who have a negative experience are far more likely to talk about it. A negative experience may even make that person less likely to see other movies with the same actors or directors.

There are many barriers to a positive experience, especially with the interactive medium. How and where people access an interactive project can be a barrier to a deep experience. Think of the different contexts in which people access websites. They may be at college or at work, and are often online in-between other aspects of their day. These audiences may be bored and seeking stimulation, but only for a short period. Then there is the home audience with more time to look around and engage. However, this space is highly subject to distraction (texts, emails, instant messages, something on TV). People in these spaces suffer from 'constant partial attention' where they are not really focused on any one aspect of technology at any one time. So, how does an interactive designer engage both of these audiences?

2.37–2.38 The World of Coca-Cola // Second Story and Donna Lawrence Productions

Second Story and Donna Lawrence Productions (US) created the interactive wall installed at the World of Coca-Cola in Atlanta, US. The wall engages participants with stories from around the world. It senses visitors close by and reacts to them, inviting them to experience the project.

As visitors interact with the wall, they are given stories from people around the world reinforcing the global Live Positively campaign and nature of the brand, whilst giving an interactive connection with people in different countries via personal stories.

2.37

2.38

2.39

2.40

Persuasion design

In researching the problem of different audiences, designers Chip and Dan Heath developed six principles of 'stickiness' – principles that can be used to make an experience 'stick' in a user's head and 'stick' on the page or app. This is important in the connected online world, because distractions and other content are only a click away. Ensuring that an audience stays with the project long enough for the client to benefit is vital when designing any interactive product. All of these principles will not fit into every project, but they should be addressed in some way during the development process. Their six principles are:

1 Simplicity
2 Unexpectedness
3 Concreteness
4 Credibility
5 Emotions
6 Stories

1 Simplicity
Make it simple (even when it's not). When designing an interactive project designers should ask themselves if the project can be summed up in one sentence. If it takes someone a few attempts to explain or contextualize the project, how is the audience going to explain it to others if they pass it on?

2 Unexpectedness
Violate expectations; designers need to take what users expect from a website or app and see if they can offer something innovative or new. This could be the interface, the theme or the aesthetic (if a pre-loader to a website is engaging, it sets up a positive reaction to the site before any content is served).

2.39–2.41
**What's your number? //
SOLID Interactive**

The Facebook app *What's your number?* from SOLID Interactive (US) fulfils many of the principles of persuasion design. It's easy to use – individuals enter their birth date and find out what their unique number is based on the world's current population. Users of the app can also link their location to their number to see where they fall in their country's population.

This app uses simplicity and surprise to push the message of the Population Action International organization. By personalizing a large number (one of 7 billion) the user becomes aware of their inclusion in the world's rapidly growing population.

56

'The app lets you enter your birth date to find out where you fall in the world's seven billion people.'

SOLID Interactive

2.41

3   *Concreteness*
The core project idea must be explicit and direct. Everyone has influences and borrows from others; designers can embrace this and use it to shore up thematic or experiential aspects of their project. Once the experience is created, designers should not deviate from the 'universe' that they have created; stay true to the aesthetic and the concept.

4   *Credibility*
Prove your credentials. When launching a new project designers have to consider that the audience may have no knowledge of the company or service that they are promoting. Inventing or incorporating ways for a new audience to engage with the service is crucial. If someone uses the app or the service and then tells their friends on Facebook or Twitter, word gets around and the product receives credibility. How should designers consider this element in the design?

5   *Emotions*
Make people care. One of the best ways to engage an audience is by making them emotionally attached to the project. Can the emotional experience come from fun or from play? Or could it come from sharing thoughts, dreams, hopes and fears with others? Have these elements been considered in the design?

6   *Stories*
Enable the audience to feel. Experiences multiply and change as they are passed from one person to another. Each time the experience is passed on, it becomes richer and deeper. What stories are the design team telling and how does this inform the user experience?

Designing experiences

User experience design (UX design) aims to design multi-sensory stimuli from which people can create their own meaningful experiences. UX design is relatively new; it emerged in part because of the advent of immersive, interactive technologies and their ability to engage beyond text and static images. An experience stays with people a lot longer than other media – it forms memories and positive associations with the product or brand.

2.42

2.42–2.45
**Natural History Museum,
LA // Second Story**

The creative team at Second Story developed interactive touch-screen experiences for visitors to the Natural History Museum of Los Angeles, US. Narrative and engagement were at the centre of the design to engage visitors with the exhibits.

UX roots
User experience design has its roots in storytelling, film and books. Its focus is really in creating an environment, product or design that takes an audience into a different state of mind outside of their ordinary life and world. This is no small task and UX designers employ a variety of methods when engaging an audience to create a compelling experience. UX design generally breaks down into four parts that form the basis for projects:

1   Distinctiveness
2   Enablement
3   Relevancy
4   Space

1   Distinctiveness
Some of the best examples of experience design are spaces, such as museums and theme parks. Every museum and theme park has a distinct environment that can only be experienced by being there and by engaging with the stories in the environment. When a visitor sees an artefact in a museum cabinet, it doesn't necessarily tell a story. The richer experience is one where interactive technology allows the story of the artefact and its owner to come alive in a meaningful and engaging way.

2.43

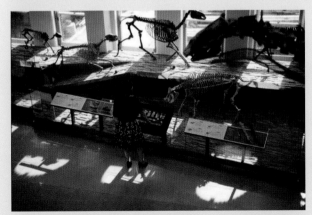

2.44

2.45

The rich media touch screens had to engage a wide variety of visitors from different age groups and backgrounds. The information had to scale based on the interest level of the user. The focus was on making the exhibits come alive to visitors in distinctive and relevant ways.

Understanding the space and the users who inhabit it is vital to delivering a successful project. Different ages require different height access, as well as varying degrees of comfort with technology. Second Story had to design accessible, inviting screens to appeal to all visitors.

2   Enablement

Story and narrative are powerful communicators, but how does a designer ensure a positive experience? The solution is in creating a more engaging interactive experience. For example, a museum exhibition on Viking artefacts would usually display a helmet or clothing with a text description and image. A better experience would be an interactive mix of video, animation and context-based information that shows the artefacts in everyday use. This would immerse the audience in the historical life of the wearer and it brings the object to life.

3   Relevancy

Part of being an interactive designer is understanding how to get into the mindset of a consumer. Designers have to be able to subtly manipulate consumers in order to make their experience as positive as possible. Designers can begin to explore what is relevant to the audience over time by delivering content and tracking what is useful to them and reacting to that feedback; it's important to involve the customer.

4   Space

Where will people be using this project? Whether it's in a museum, in Disneyland or in a bedroom, the design has to try to accommodate those spaces. The ability to think through how an audience will engage with the project is important. If the project calls for a touch screen in a museum, designers will need to allow for the different heights of users (a display that was five feet high from the floor would prevent an eight year old from using it). On-site visits are crucial to map where to best place the project for maximum impact (what is the space's traffic flow? Where do most people stand when viewing an exhibit or ride?).

Experiences are as unique as the people connecting with them and so are not understood in the same way by everyone. Even so, by considering as many angles as possible, by incorporating design passions and by learning from research, interactive designers should be able to produce an experience that people will relate to positively – that's the goal of every project.

2.46–2.49 Visit México // Studio La Flama and JWT

Tourism México commissioned J. Walter Thompson (JWT) (Mexico) to create a stunning, engaging and memorable video campaign for North America. Luis Torres directed the video sequences that ran on the digital billboards of American Eagle Outfitters in Times Square, New York. The challenge was in using the uneven spaces and surfaces of the billboards on the building for the most impact. Luis used colour, animation, text and rich imagery to communicate the natural beauty of Mexico as a juxtaposition against the urban grittiness of NYC.

2.46

2.47

2.48

2.49

Interview:
Lydia Swangren,
UX designer

Lydia Swangren is a user experience (UX) designer from Chicago, Illinois, US, with an extensive background in interactive projects.

What is a UX designer?

An experience designer (or user-experience designer/ user-experience architect) helps define the various user touch points and framework of a product and designs how it is to be perceived, learned and used. Typically, experience designers work within the realm of a person's interaction with a computer screen.

It is important to understand that experience design is a highly multidisciplinary field, and it is a collaborative role. Many different disciplines fall within its spectrum, including: user research, content development, information architecture, user-centred design, interface and interactive design, creative design, branding and technical development.

What is important about designing experiences for a client?

Users are more likely to trust and engage with organizations that create compelling, memorable and well-executed holistic experiences; a well-designed experience is a reflection of the business it represents. Experience design considers all touch points users have with a product and employs a process to ensure consistency and quality; and this helps to produce the best outcome.

How do you approach designing an experience when working on a project?

My first step is to become familiar with the project. I need to learn about its scope, the target users, platform, functional and technical requirements. I try to find the sweet spot between the user needs and goals, and the business goals. I design through an iterative process that spans the entire project life cycle, from the initial sketching phase through to the launch.

How important are personas and scenarios to the development of a project?

I use **personas and scenarios** whenever I have the opportunity to do so; both are very useful on large-scale projects. Personas and scenarios humanize impersonal customer demographics and help the project team to stay focused on a common set of goals and needs.

Scenarios are useful in the exploratory and discovery phase of a project and help to define how users are going to complete a task before the interface is fully designed. A scenario can help the designer validate the design and assumptions using a real-life narrative. For example, 'Is the task flow realistic in supporting the user's needs in accomplishing and reaching the desired end goal?' (See chapter 3 for more information about personas and scenarios.)

What metrics (measurements) do you use to qualify a positive user experience?

A few **metrics** that qualify a positive user experience for a website or application product or service include the following:

- Does the experience provide value to its target users with fresh, relevant content with the expected functionality? Is it done well?
- Is the site or application easy and a pleasure to use?
- Does the design reduce user effort?
- Is the application pleasant to view? Is it representative and supportive of the brand?
- Does the site or application evoke trust? Will users hesitate to complete their tasks or provide necessary information for any reason?
- Is the site or application technology appropriate and responsive?

What is the future of experience design as a discipline?

Demand for experience design practitioners will continue to grow rapidly. As systems become increasingly complex, multidisciplinary experience design teams are needed to collaborate and create the best-integrated, cross-platform experiences.

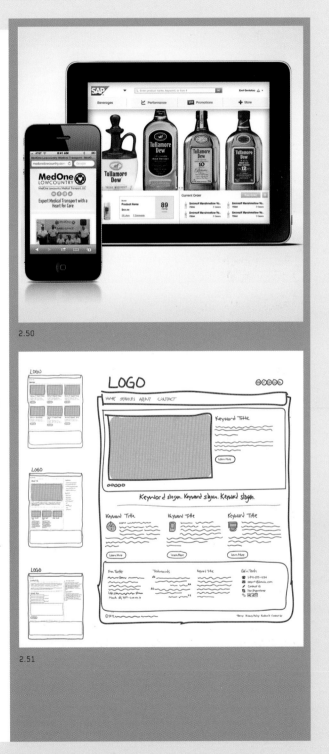

2.50

2.51

2.50–2.51 UX design // Multi-platform

User experience is not restricted to one space, or one technology. Designers have to think about and design an experience across multiple screens and user spaces. A product may go from a website on a monitor to a tablet and then a smartphone, the UX designer has to ensure that the consumer has the ability to engage with the product seamlessly and positively.

Images courtesy of Emil Picasso Gentolizo
<MobileAndTabletSolutions.com>

Case study: Multi-platform delivery

Studio: SOLID Interactive, US
Client: Film Fresh

Film Fresh is an indie-based film distribution company located in Hollywood, CA, US. SOLID Interactive were tasked with integrating a digital video-on-demand service to replace the DivX-based offering that was available on their website.

The brief

SOLID Interactive's brief from Film Fresh was in two parts: to revamp Film Fresh's website, and to develop a Flash-based video service that allowed customers to watch on-demand video on their web browsers and Android-based tablets (via an application).

The Android application (app) was to be designed and developed by SOLID from the ground up. The idea was to use some of the elements from existing apps that they had built to create an intuitive and easy-to-use interface.

For the web-based part of the project, the interactive design team worked with a third-party design and UX group to implement the changes to the web application, and then designed the Flash player to fit the look and feel of the existing site. Both teams needed to create an integrated experience that would flow between the browser-based store, the video player and the Android app.

The pre-development process

The web application required SOLID to work with the third-party team to determine the key components and updates for the integration of the new service. Meetings were held with both teams studying UX documents, reviewing mock-up design, and deciding what the best options were from a technical, consumer and business perspective. Once the specifications were finalized, the team at SOLID used the design documents as the basis for the development of the Android app.

Firstly, the views that were to be included in the app were mapped. Each section was broken down into a detailed set of wireframes; it's these wireframes that inform the information architecture (IA). This visual architecture became the blueprint for the project.

2.52

Tapping anywhere in the black area takes users to title details.

Box art grid scrolls vertically. Tapping box art in the grid takes user straight to title details.

2.53

2.52–2.54 Wireframes // Film Fresh

Wireframes set out the functionality or architecture of a site. This is vitally important because bringing in art assets too early can lock in the look of a site or project before any of the interactions have been planned.

In this carousel concept, the box art in the grid lights up one-by-one (left to right). As each lights up, the large box art and title information slide in from the right.

2.54

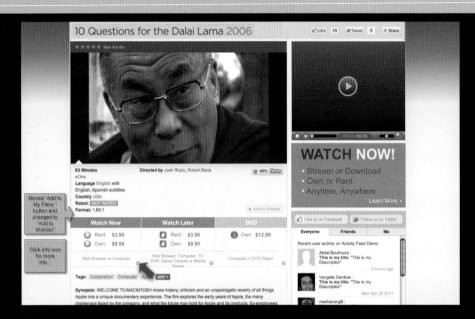

2.55–2.56
Design prototypes

As the design process moves on the design team will create several variations of layouts with art assets to get a better sense of how the site will look. As Film Fresh was going to operate from a computer monitor to a mobile screen, the designs had to look consistent across these platforms.

2.55

The production process

Once the master documents were created, the implementation of the website and tablet app began. As resources were assigned to the separate projects, the team worked through the technical requirements. The technical tasks were split across the website and the tablet app.

The website

The team implemented a content service that was the backbone of the web store. There were many existing touch points (the point of contact between a customer and a service) in the application that needed to be replaced to complete the project. These modifications created changes in the flow of the application that allowed users to take advantage of some of the innovative features available with the new service. Then, the team integrated the new services and designs.

The next phase was testing and quality assurance using an experienced group of analysts to ensure that all the elements, new and old, worked properly.

The tablet app

The Android app was one of the first of its kind to use the chosen content service. Because of this, the team had to ensure that all technical areas were thoroughly thought out and that all functional requirements were in line with the capabilities of the back-end **application programming interface** (API).

As the app's functionality was broken down, a list of technical tasks were assigned to a team of developers to code.

The development process for the Android app required the team to be flexible enough to prototype small sections while building the entire application. This was a departure from SOLID's standard process; senior engineers were brought in to oversee the entire app so that the team had experts on hand to discuss technical issues. SOLID's QA (quality assurance) group were also heavily involved through the entire process and were able to test parts of the app as it was being developed.

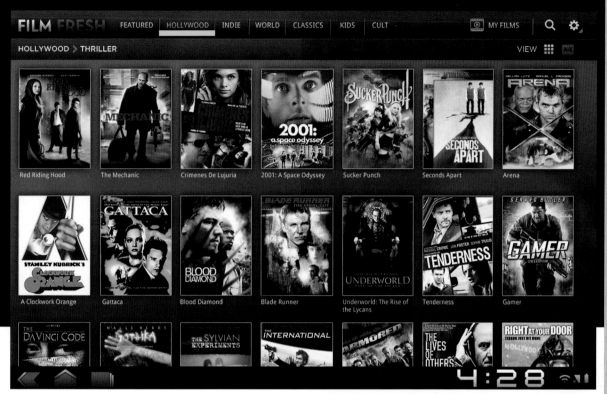

2.56

The launch
The website and the Android app had a great response. Film Fresh has featured SOLID Interactive's work at the 2012 Consumer Electronics Show (CES) and the Sundance Film Festival. The users are very happy with the ability to rent and purchase high-quality films across many platforms. SOLID Interactive continue to upgrade and develop new features for the website and the Android app, as well as implementing the Film Fresh store onto other portable and set-box platforms.

PROJECT TOOLS
- Adobe Flash Builder (development)
- Adobe Illustrator (design)
- Adobe Photoshop (design)
- Eclipse IDE (development)
- Google Docs (collaboration and spec writing)
- Microsoft PowePoint (wireframe/UI presentation)
- OmniGraffle (wireframes)
- Redmine (bug tracking and project management)
- Smartsheet (project management)

Project: Engage through interactivity

The brief

Create an experience for a deeper level of engagement in a museum exhibition. Increasingly, museums have employed interactive design to facilitate deeper learning and interaction with its exhibits. Museums are difficult spaces to design for because the audience is very broad and the purpose of a museum is to educate and inform.

1 Research

Visit a museum or exhibition and get to know the space. Document your museum/exhibition space and sketch out potential approaches towards a deeper experience. Take photographs of areas that could be improved to support your analysis (ensure that you are allowed to do this!). The document will outline your plan for the project explaining ideas, concepts, colours, experiences, ambiance and audience interactions. The document must contain a minimum of ten pages of content, including images, sketches and text.

Considerations

- Visit the museum many times to get a sense of the exhibition and who visits it; if possible, on different days.

- The documentation will become your reference for the entire project, so ensure it's detailed enough to guide your process.

2 Sketching the experience

Choose one exhibit or special exhibition (for example the dinosaur hall in a natural history museum or a collection of paintings) and create an outline of the interactive experience of the exhibition. Create a **click-through** wireframe of your concept and its installation in the space.

Create several slides/pages of drawings and images that show the installation. From the entrance point to the exhibition hall, show navigation of the space and interaction with the technology (surfaces, navigational interfaces and audio or visuals).

Considerations

■   What technologies will work well in this space? If the solution is for touch screens in the main hall, what does the interface look like?

■   How do people interact with your concept and what will they see? If there is sound will it spill out into the other areas and annoy other museum users?

3 Prototype

Develop a multimedia presentation showcasing your final refined concept using art assets such as video and photos. The presentation could be created using PowerPoint or Flash. The presentation should be a development from your wireframes and sketches and include:

(a)   The traffic (people) flow of the space – how will people move through the space within the new installation?

(b)   The navigation of devices such as touch screens, tablets or an MP3 player with audio – how do people know which button to press and how will they access the content?

(c)   An overview of the experience you are proposing – what will make this a more rewarding and engaging visit for the audience? Why should the museum invest in your idea?

Considerations

■   Should the experience be portable or locked down (touch screens or video screens at the exhibits)?

■   Would using location-sensitive sensors allow the application to track the visitor and provide them with content based on where they are in the museum?

■   Are there projected/interactive environments?

Tips!

1   Think about the users. Don't assume you are the audience.

2   Will the wireframe make sense to everyone?

3   Spend time on the art assets, they sell the project.

4   Think big. Attempt to amaze.

3.1

Chapter 3: The Industry Process

The pitch

In this chapter, we explore an important part of the industry process – pitching a design to a potential client. We examine industry best practices and the relationship between the designer and the client, as well as the process of moving from pitch to project.

Most people are aware of the idea of a project 'pitch', for example the TV series *Dragons' Den* (UK) and *Shark Tank* (US) show people making pitches. Pitches are competitive, and can be nerve-wracking. Most art and design students have first-hand experience of presenting to a room full of people.

Critiques of projects or work-in-progress presentations are all excellent preparation for delivering a pitch. Although it's not always obvious, learning how to best present ideas and being able to talk about work to others is an opportunity to hone the skills necessary to deal with a client pitch.

Pitch types
There are two kinds of pitches (or proposals): the competitive pitch known as 'RFPs' (request for proposals) and the invitational pitch.

1   *The request for proposal (RFP)*
    Most studios are going to be involved in a request for a proposal. An RFP is a document sent by the client that outlines, often in detail, what outcomes they require. The studio then creates materials to answer the brief, and sends them to the client. This is a sort of blind taste test; there is no communication with the client, so the answer to the RFP has to stand on its own merits. If the materials are interesting to the client, the design studio is asked to prepare for a meeting with the client to pitch their idea.

2   *The invitational pitch*
    The invitational pitch often occurs when the studio already has a relationship with the client and is invited to come up with a design solution for a brief; or the client may have been impressed by the studio's previous work and invites them to a meeting. These kinds of briefs are often less formal and much less competitive. Even so, the client needs to be impressed and the pitch delivered in much the same way as for a competitive 'open' call for proposals.

Preparation for a pitch meeting

When a studio has decided to go after a brief, the first essential action is to research the client, their brand and products. A small team is assembled to create pitch materials, and possibly prototypes, based on this research. When a team is developing and researching materials for a pitch there are many considerations, here are a few essential ones:

1   Who is the client? What is their business?
2   What is the product/service they are looking to promote?
3   Which advertising or launch campaigns have they used in the past?
4   Does what we do as a studio fit in with what the client expects?

The briefs can be very ephemeral or very explicit; studios adapt their research depending on what is required of them. Pitching can be a resource-intensive and expensive process.

A controversial issue is that some clients may ask for speculative (or 'spec') work in advance of a meeting. This is when a client asks a studio to send or bring working prototypes of their ideas to a meeting. Spec work has a history of making design studios uncomfortable; in essence, the client is asking the studio to spend a lot of time and money preparing for a job that they may not get. Many studios refuse to undertake spec work because of this.

Post-pitch: the aftermath

So, what happens after the pitch meeting? If the pitch is successful, the studio wins the contract, money changes hands and work begins. If the pitch is unsuccessful, every hour of research, artwork and interactive prototypes could be regarded as wasted. However, a studio will use a failed pitch as part of the learning process. Usually, there's a post-mortem after the pitch when the team discusses what went right and what went wrong.

3.2

3.3

3.4

3.2–3.4 Televisa pitch // Studio La Flama

These stills are from a pitch video created by Luis Torres of Studio La Flama for the Mexican TV channel Televisa. The concept was to tap into the massive popularity of the *Lucha Libre* and its masked wrestlers. The textures of the dolls (characters based on a prototype kids' TV show) were rough with canvas, leather and visible stitching. The environments were aesthetically clean and vibrant, providing visual contrast to the dolls.

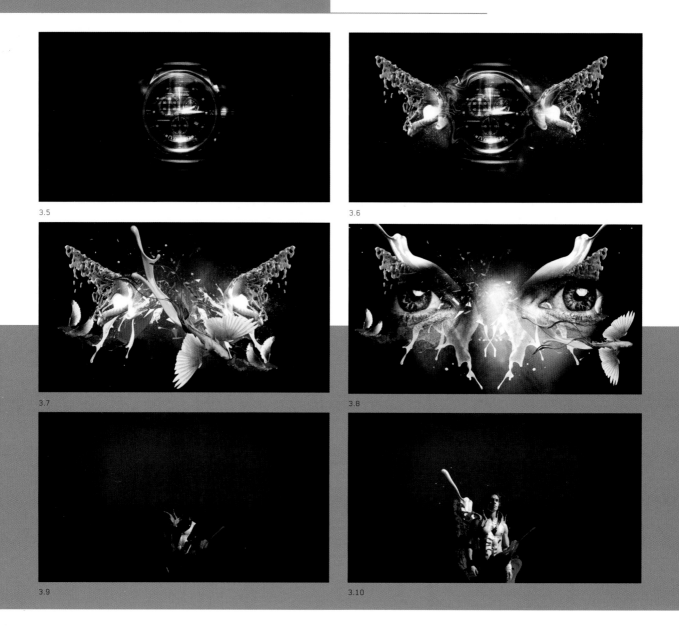

3.5

3.6

3.7

3.8

3.9

3.10

3.5–3.12 Citizen pitch // Studio La Flama

Studio La Flama (Luis Torres, director) created this pitch working with JWT, Mexico. Citizen Watch Ltd wanted a visually driven TV commercial for their watches. Torres worked with a strong acrylic and oil-based paint aesthetic that implied movement, grace and a dreamlike state. As the client wanted an artistic feel, the visuals quickly took on a surreal style based on movement, dreams and time.

3.11

3.12

Interview: David Burrows, design consultant

David Burrows has been involved in online advertising for over 15 years. He spent five years at Yahoo! Inc as European Head of Ad Technology and has worked in several creative agencies and advertising start-ups. He's been involved in many successful online campaigns for clients such as Ford, Sony, Warner Brothers and Electronic Arts.

Do you feel there is an art to a successful pitch? If so, how do you hone that art?

Pitches are fundamentally about communication, and communication is an art with many styles. There are plenty of hit songs sung by less-than-great voices, and so it is with pitches. Horrible pitches with a good idea can be successful. Terrible ideas pitched by great presenters can be successful, but then you're stuck with having to implement a terrible idea!

For a great pitch you need to forget all the extraneous stuff and concentrate on having a strong idea and communicating it to the best of your ability.

How critical is research into the client's business? How much of this do you put into your pitch?

You need to understand your client to communicate effectively. A commercial pitch is always about solving the client's problem and you need to understand them to solve it – a great idea that doesn't solve the client's problem is useless. The more you know about their company, market and environment the better.

How important is it to build a relationship with a client?

A pitch can be won by just building a relationship with the client. Sometimes the idea might not fit but your approach and 'look and feel' is right and you'll get the job. Unfortunately, this is hard to plan for; the worst thing you can do is pretend you're a very different person to who you really are, just to win the pitch. Relationships are a two-way street; make sure you choose the pitches that are a good fit for your company and its capabilities.

Do you prepare several solutions to an initial brief or is it all-or-nothing?

One of the most important aspects to a presentation is confidence. Unless there's a very good reason or the client has asked specifically to see several ideas, it's best to go all-in with your best shot. Spend time and resources on your one best idea rather than preparing several approaches and diluting the impact.

Do you have any essential tips for successful approaches to the pitch?

There are definitely a few essential things you should do to prepare before pitching to a client.

- The idea is the key, you have to present professionally and with enthusiasm to really get your point across.
- Do your research; make sure you understand the client as fully as possible.

- Pitch to the client, not yourselves – put yourselves in the client's shoes – what do they need to know?
- Your pitch is a story; make it engaging and structure it properly: beginning, middle and end.
- Rewrite, rewrite, rewrite. Edit your pitch until it is as concise as possible; the shorter the better.
- Pitches are conversations, treat them like one. You are not here to tell the client what to think, you are putting across an idea. Allocate time in the presentation to engage in conversation, so it's not just about you.
- Practise! Run through the pitch as many times as you can with colleagues. The more times you do it, the better; you'll feel more relaxed when presenting and practice builds confidence.

Are there practices to avoid, ones that you may have used in the past and have learnt not to use again?

- Read the brief! Really read it. Many pitches have been lost by misunderstanding the brief. Have other members of the team read it too? Get a consensus of what the client may be looking for. Your interpretation may only make sense to you.

- Stop talking and listen! Don't ignore, interrupt or talk over clients. It's their money and if communication is good, you stand a much better chance of getting the job.
- Be concise. If it's hard to explain your idea, it's probably a bad idea. Don't think that a good pitch presentation with fantastic artwork and media will hide any cracks in your thinking.
- Slow down! The number one problem in public speaking is talking too fast. This can make the speaker appear nervous, unsure and hard to understand.
- Death by PowerPoint. Images and slides are aids, not a focus. Keep slides to a minimum.
- No life stories. Keep credentials short, you are already in the door; you don't need to give clients a 20-minute talk on how you got there.
- No techno-babble. The pitch is not the place to discuss technical details.
- Don't lecture. Clients are looking for solutions not a discussion about their mistakes or how they don't 'get' it.

3.13–3.14   Content delivery pitch // David Burrows

These images are taken from a pitch presentation outlining the proposed solution to a client brief to deliver multi-platform content to consumers. The images are simple and communicated themes and ideas to the client in a focused and manageable manner.

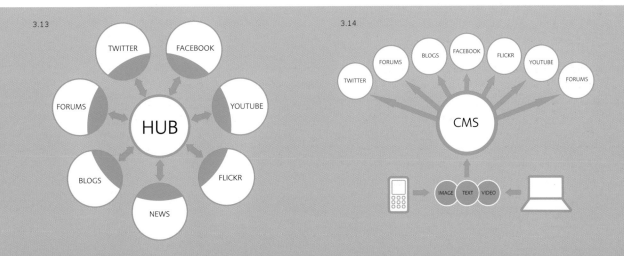

3.13

3.14

Art direction and aesthetic

Once a pitch has been accepted, managerial direction is required to help develop the idea into something tangible and workable. When creating products such as video games, websites or interactive installations, it is the job of an art director and project leader to communicate to the team the next steps involved in moving the project forward.

Roles and titles

The art director leads the team and ensures that the team members adhere to the brief and to any aspects of the brief that are restricted (for example, use of the client logo, colours that the project may have to use or cannot use). The art director supervises all aspects of the project. For example, a project team may include smaller teams of graphic designers, animators, programmers, interface specialists, interaction designers and a project manager. The art director guides all of these people towards a common goal and project completion.

Interactive design studio roles

In interactive design, many skill sets can overlap; here are some examples of the main jobs that you would find in an interactive studio.

Creative director: responsible for communicating project goals into tangible design solutions and establishing the conceptual and stylistic direction for the design teams. Creative directors are also supervisors and administrators ensuring the correct resources and staff are in place.

Art director: responsible for working with the team on production and making decisions on the development of content and driving the interactivity and aesthetic of the project.

Lead designer/project leader: responsible for managing and coordinating with everyone involved in the production of a project. This is more of an administrative role.

Project manager/producer: responsible for coordinating and administrating individual projects. A project manager works on scheduling and budget development, procures outside assets or technology, and works closely with the client and the team.

Technical director: responsibilities include developing a technical strategy, assessing the technical risk of a project and assessing new technologies. He/she communicates with the project manager and runs the technical team of operations and back-end staff.

Technical lead: responsible for overseeing the programming and hardware and software aspects of the project. Usually a senior member of the development team with experience of a wide array of projects, who can direct the development team as well as produce content.

Visual designer/designer: catch-all title for a person working on the project, the designer could be coding, creating art assets and interfaces or testing for usability. Small companies may use this one-size-fits-all title.

Front-end developer: responsible for utilizing web or interactive technologies and scripting languages to create assets based on illustrations, wireframes, **HTML** markup and **CSS** provided by the design team. Front-end developers create scripts that affect the look, aesthetic and interaction of the project (e.g. CSS scripts that create the layout of a website or the ActionScript in Flash that makes an advergame work).

Back-end developer: programmers who work with web-server systems, databases, web applications and Application Programming Interfaces (APIs). For example, if the project needed to use technology from Google, the back-end developer would create or modify a Google API.

Usability designer/consultant: a similar title to the information architecture (IA)/user experience (UX) designer. A usability design consultant works with the team to measure, test or design the project from the user perspective.

Motion/video designer: responsible for development of production and **post-production** of motion-based imagery for the project. These can also be used to create materials for presentation to clients.

Writer/copywriter/editor: responsible for writing, editing and proofreading narratives, editorials and story text for the project.

Interface/user interface designer: responsible for creating all interfaces for the project; works closely with the usability designer and art directors to ensure the interface is usable, efficient and works with the aesthetic of the project.

Operations (technical): IT personnel who set up hardware and software, install servers and mission critical communications. These people ensure everything that the project runs on actually works.

Operations manager/director: responsible for issues with finances, human resources, contracts and legal matters, technology resources and facilities. Also oversees project management and connects project-level finances with the overall performance of the studio. Financial and administrative staff report to the operations manager.

Testing: depending on the size of the project, the testing team may be one person or several people. The role is to try to break the project and test for any unforeseen errors or mistakes in development.

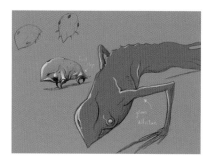

3.15

Prototype and iteration

Once the research is complete, work on prototypes begins. Prototyping early and often during the project allows the team to make radical decisions and changes to a project before it's too late or too expensive to change. It's important for designers to know that you can connect X with Y before the project progresses. The point of the prototype is to prove it can be done. This is a critical phase for experimentation and project development.

Creating a fast and 'dirty' prototype is the best way to prove a concept is tenable. This prototype is then reproduced and added to. This process is called iteration (sometimes also known as versioning, as many versions of a prototype are made).

Projects can very quickly become complex and, therefore, can very quickly become expensive. Building prototypes that work prove the task can be achieved, which is a boost for the team, and reassuring for the client. For example, it might only be a box that interacts with another rectangle, but it's a proof of concept (another industry standard phrase) that the intended interaction can happen.

3.16

Development and testing

The next step is development and testing, usability and (sometimes) user testing. A solid and informed approach to development and testing is central to the success of any interactive project. The team has to prove to the client that its ideas are viable and that an audience will use them. Testing during development is used in all interactive industries. It is important to encourage non-technical people to use the prototype and learn from that process. This feedback is used to hone the project.

Choke points

Feedback might, for example, discover the 'choke points'. These are areas where the project might slow down because there is too much going on, or if too many people access a website at once; this is also known as 'load testing'. Why did the project hang there or who would have thought someone would use the interface like that?

The early bugs (unexpected errors in the coding of the project) come out in testing and solidify the design choices for the final project.

As prototypes are developed, more rigorous testing will occur. It is vital that the project discover errors while testing rather than when it is live.

In the next case study, we again visit the Specialmoves studio and see how they developed an idea and tested it for World Wrestling Entertainment (currently the largest professional wrestling organization in the world) in a viral campaign to promote WrestleMania XXVII.

3.17

3.15–3.17 Arizona Department of Health Services // Studio La Flama

These are preliminary sketches for an animation Studio La Flama created for the Arizona Department of Health Services. The brief was to create a creature that would represent addiction. The development began with a comic-book style aesthetic, but as the animation process developed the creature and its environment (the inside of a teenager's body) became more biological, stylized and reminiscent of a sci-fi movie.

Case study: WrestleMania viral campaign

Studio: Specialmoves, UK
Client: WWE/Sports Revolution

Specialmoves created a social media campaign for the launch of WrestleMania XXVII.

The concept

With WrestleMania XXVII on the horizon, World Wrestling Entertainment (WWE) wanted a social-media asset to create some extra digital buzz around the event. Specialmoves had already successfully created a **viral** Facebook-based marketing campaign for the TV series *Misfits*. The concept was to create an experience that would connect wrestling fans with the stars of WWE. The campaign would take participating fans' names and Facebook profile pictures, and composite them in a short clip promoting WrestleMania. WWE is all about larger-than-life personas, and the best way to involve fans was to include them in a custom backstage video with some of the most popular WWE Superstars.

The planning stage

The project had to feel like a user had tuned in to a normal TV clip, so everything was shot live, and for authenticity, the clip had to star the actual WWE Superstars. After meeting to agree on the concept, the WWE promo team penned the base script. They knew the brand well and created weekly plots for the show, so it was essential that they controlled the TV production. The piece had to feel as 'real' as possible. Research showed that placing the fan backstage was the key, so the WWE team wrote the script accordingly – providing a framework for the designers.

Prototyping for WrestleMania

Based on their experience with the *Misfits* campaign the studio knew that for this project, the main interaction occurs behind the scenes. There are many other campaigns and apps that ask users to upload a picture and then they have to manually position their eyes, nose, mouth and so on. This is usually due to technological limitations, not a usability decision, but it's a barrier to a rewarding and efficient experience. The team felt that by being clever in **compositing** the user's photo, they could simplify the experience for the fan – the easier it is for them the more likely they are to want to use the product. The usability process for the project would be for a fan to visit the site (click), accept the Facebook permissions (click), and press Go! (click – three clicks for the entire experience to work). There would be no bothersome menus and tools in the way of what's essentially a fun and engaging experience for the fans.

The other benefit was that by not showing the users exactly what Facebook elements would be used, there would be more of a surprise when seeing their photo on an animated TV screen, or on the front page of a newspaper in the video clip.

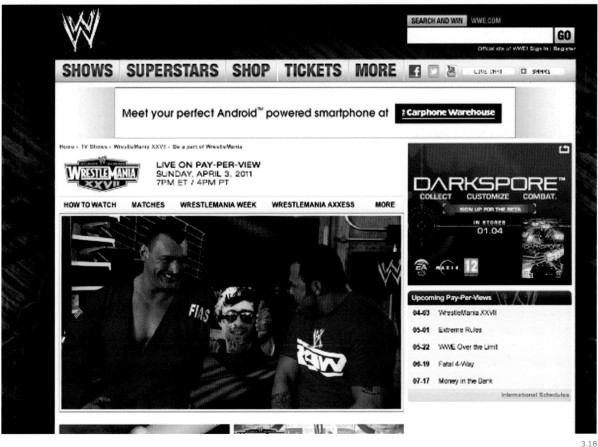

3.18

3.18 The Facebook campaign

By featuring actual WWE Superstars, the interactive video brought fans up close and personal with their heroes.

3.19 Usability testing

Special attention is paid to how users interact with the online interface through a series of usability tests.

3.19

3.20

3.20 Image composition tests

Test compositions showing how the Facebook image integration works. The WWE Stars were shot with chroma-green props. Using Flash, the green areas were keyed out, leaving space for the fans' Facebook assets.

Integration

It was imperative that the Facebook image integration be impeccable, otherwise the overall impact would be lost. The magic isn't in just seeing your image pasted in a video, it's seeing it look real and part of the shot. Visual effects are best used to help tell a story; as soon as the effects become too obvious, the audience loses its focus on the larger narrative.

The best experiences are so well designed that people just 'use' the end product and don't have to wrestle with unnecessary tools. Using skills gained on the *Misfits* shoot, the visual effects designer was able to guide the TV production team and WWE Superstars in LA to get the shots that were needed, making the integration look seamless.

3.21

3.21 Camera motion

When shooting the VFX shots, lighting and camera angles were locked off to ease the initial post-production work. Towards the end of development, natural camera motion was added back to match the regular shots.

3.22

3.22 Post-production

The team used Apple Shake for the post-production compositing. Textures and effects were added to sit on top of the Facebook images; e.g. paper creases and lighting gradients.

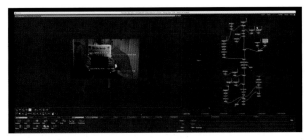

3.23

3.23 Motion tracking

Motion tracking was essential as the Facebook images would have to move to match the video. Apple Shake's automated tracking, together with a little manual tweaking, achieved a precise end result.

Project management and deadlines

Though the project was small in terms of UX (compared to a multi-lingual website), the studio created a complete UX flow and wireframes to help the client to firmly grasp what would be created, and act as a foundation for the WWE graphic designers to work from. Organization and deadlines were critical as the studio were dealing with a large multinational business with restricted access to their talent. The producer and project manager had to work closely to make sure everything would be in place at the right time to get the project finished. The deadline for the project was tight, but manageable. Here's a breakdown of the basic steps from start to finish:

- Initial script was written by the WWE team.
- Script was tweaked and finalized by all parties.
- One-day shoot at the Honda Centre in Los Angeles (WWE team and the visual effects designer supervised the shots from a visual effects – VFX – perspective).
- Video editing into the final piece with music by the WWE editors.
- UX flow and wireframes created.
- Visual effects mock-ups designed (how each FX shot should look).
- The interface was built using Adobe Flash so a Flash framework had to be planned and built.
- The video clips were optimized for use in Flash (keying, point tracking, colour grading).
- The clips were integrated into framework using the Flash compositing tool.
- The art assets were added – this included the menu/interface designs and graphics to the app (WWE and Specialmoves).
- The programmers created the linkage between the live Facebook user data and the Flash framework.
- Once all this was complete the WWE and Specialmoves project was launched!

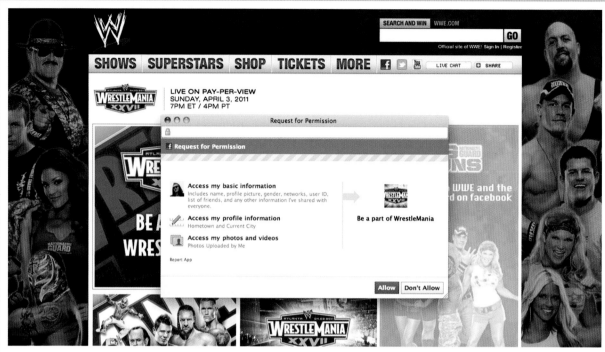

3.24

3.25

3.24–3.25 Social media

Social media forms the basis of
the success of this campaign.
Connecting through Facebook,
fans can personalize their video
and share it with their friends.

3.26

3.26 Visual integration

This series of mock-ups was used as an initial proof of concept that the compositions had all worked well and were seamlessly integrating into the video.

The reaction

The project was launched on WWE.com and was immediately embraced by WWE fans, with over 300,000 views and over 40,000 Facebook shares in less than three weeks after the launch. The fans' enthusiasm meant that the film spread like wildfire and made this a successful experience.

PROJECT TOOLS

- Pens and notebooks (initial idea planning and sketching throughout the project build)
- Adobe Flash (app build)
- Adobe Photoshop (visual effects graphics, mock-ups and screen designs)
- Apple Final Cut Pro (video clip trimming and preparation)
- Apple QuickTime Pro (video playback and quick trimming)
- Apple Shake (visual effects, compositing and colour grading)
- Apple TextEdit (keyframe notes)
- Custom-built C++ Keyframe Generator (for translating the keyframe notes into actionscript classes)
- Facebook API (for connecting the app with Facebook)

Project: Create a campaign pitch

The brief

Rough Guides is a leading publisher of travel guides aimed at student and budget travellers. Imagine that they are launching a new travel service for their website and mobile content. Travellers can use the guides to get information about a destination then book it directly with Rough Guides travel. The service must be aimed at the core Rough Guides audience or low-budget, young travellers.

1 Research and wireframe

Research the competition (e.g. Lonely Planet, Footprint and Let's Go) and come up with sketches of a site that would appeal to younger, budget-oriented travellers, who are more interested in experiences over luxury and tourist hotspots. Create a wireframe of the site concentrating on visual impact, ease of use and ease of navigation (what things do these travellers want most?).

Considerations

- Rough Guides is a well-established brand – what can be done to connect that identity to the travel-service website?

- For wireframes concentrate on the intended audience – young, adventurous and more likely to have digital tools, such as smartphones and tablets.

- When researching other competitors' websites, think about what works and what doesn't. What do you think is most important to the Rough Guides' traveller and what can be jettisoned?

2 Pitch the concept

Create a presentation that you would use to pitch your idea to the Rough Guides team. It's important to establish a mood and an artistic aesthetic that relates to their brand. Use PowerPoint or other multimedia creation software as part of the pitch. Explain how the service will work and what separates it from the competition. Create art assets/images and media that will persuade the Rough Guides board to take on your concept for the website.

Considerations

- The pitch needs to be concise, inspiring and passionate. Ensure that you get the client excited about your idea.

- The pitch materials need to show that you have researched the company and its customer base and that you understand their marketplace and identity.

- The interactive elements need to be slick and accessible, this is not the place to overload the client with technical details. Remember, you're selling the aesthetics and the concept (but make sure that the client understands how the website would work for users).

Tips!

1 Stay focused. Don't over design the interface.
2 Practise the presentation in front of colleagues and listen to their feedback.
3 Would your ideas also apply to mobile or apps? You might want to consider these platforms in your pitch.
4 Throw in some unusual and crazy ideas!

Chapter 4: Audience, Usability and Testing

Designers have to consider the audience and how easy the interface is to use and balance that with rigorous testing to ensure the application doesn't fail when used over and over again.

Design for the audience

This chapter explores ways in which to engage the audience. It looks at the importance of usability as well as examining the other elements of interactive design that bring the entire project together. The first section examines the use of personas and scenarios in order to attract users to an interactive campaign.

'Personas work because they tell stories.'

Whitney Quesenbery, user experience expert

User personas

Designers need a method of guiding their design decisions in line with the intended audience. This is where personas and scenarios are used. The persona is a created 'person' who becomes the benchmark used for the project. It's enticing to create a shallow persona instead of a well thought-out member of the project demographic audience. Christine Perfetti (CEO of Perfetti Media) sums up the persona usage problem: 'Imagine that you are a shoe designer. To design for all users, it's logical to design a shoe that satisfies the needs of the average person. The average male's shoe size is 8 $^1/_4$. So, as a designer, would you build all of your shoes to fit only the average man? Probably not.'

A persona is not a magic bullet that allows a design team to jump into the minds of the masses, instead it's an approach towards a deeper consideration of an audience. There is still some discussion in the design field about the usefulness of the persona, the following are some of the positive and negative considerations.

The pros and cons of user personas

The upside of personas:

1   They establish common needs and goals for a disparate audience.
2   If a designer needs to add a new feature, they can refer to the persona to assess its usefulness.
3   Personas can streamline the production process, for example, it can target different users, so a project aimed at children and parents might be a different audience to teenagers or older people.
4   Personas can be a useful evaluation guide; the designers can refer to the personas as a method of avoiding intensive usability testing.

The downside of personas:

1   Personas potentially lead to an artificial sense of understanding of users, which may mislead the team development process.
2   Personas are not real people and so can't talk back and ask questions; they are fictitious and artificial.
3   Personas may be a composite of a demographic-based audience; they lack distinction and individuality.

No system is perfect and personas are a tool that can help. It's up to the team and the art director to decide on their effectiveness. For young designers starting out, personas can be very useful for 'thinking of what the audience needs'.

The scenario

A scenario situates a persona in the process of using a product to assess its functional and aesthetic quality. For example, the team may have prototyped a new navigation interface for a website and would then ask, 'How would the persona Jackie use this? Would she want to?' and then in the scenario, 'Is Jackie going through the process of engaging with the application?'

The scenario adds context to the persona. It takes a bit of imagination, but the scenario is the story of the persona using the design. Scenarios break down into two elements: the evocative and the prescriptive.

1   Evocative scenarios relate to the experience of the project. They describe the feeling and emotions related to the desired outcome of the project. For example, 'How does Jackie feel when she sees this page layout?'

2   Prescriptive scenarios are the details of the design, for example, 'What happens when Jackie clicks on this?'

Think about a scenario as a storyboard that takes the persona through part of the project. A storyboard helps clients to see how consumers use applications. Scenarios help to solve specific problems and minimize the risk of finding out that the project is not going to work for the audience. Giving the persona a voice and detailed scenario pre-empts the need for expensive user testing, which is especially important if the project has a small budget.

Usability in design: rules and principles

Usability in design is the process of designing a product so that the audience can use it easily and intuitively. So how does a team design for usability? The answer is to always consider the audience, which is difficult if the audience is different from the make-up of the design team.

Interactive design teams need to continually check to see if one feature changing affects the overall usability of the product. There are some general principles of usability in design that help to keep the project easy to use and run efficiently.

The eight rules of interface design

When developing any interface for a project there are fundamentals to consider. In his book *Designing the User Interface*, Ben Shneiderman (professor at the University of Maryland), proposed 'Eight Golden Rules of Interface Design'. They work well for interfaces and should be considered when designing an interactive project.

1   *Be consistent*
    Consistency is important when designing an interface or application.
    For example, on a website, a company logo is normally a link back to the front page. If this linkage changes based on where the user is within the site, it's confusing.

2   *Use shortcuts for frequent users*
    If a website or application has content that people return to often, make it easy for them to get to that content. For example, news sites allow users to choose the subjects they're interested in, and sites such as Amazon.com store credit card details so customers don't have to constantly re-enter the same information.

3   *Design informative feedback*
    Feedback is a crucial part of the overall experience. For example, on a web page the text loads first and quickly, rich media loads slowly (e.g. videos), so ensure that the initial content has some value. A large media site may take a long time to load, so use pre-loader animations to show the user that something is happening.

4   *Design navigation or dialogue with conclusions*
A four-page news article, for example, should have a navigation system that links to pages 1, 2, 3 and 4. It should indicate which page users are on, so they can easily go backwards and forwards in the article, but also know the article's length.

5   *Design informative errors*
Websites should be designed so that if a link is broken or a page is missing the 'error' (known as the '404 error' page) that is displayed is informative. Users should be able to navigate back to the main site and the error page should be considered as content in line with the aesthetics of the site.

6   *Design an 'undo' option*
Anyone using a large website should always be able to get back to a previous page, track where they have been or move to the front page. Many web pages use a feature called 'breadcrumbs', which is a dynamic set of text links under the main navigation that allow users to track back to earlier content areas.

7   *Design for individuality*
People relate best to systems that they find easy to use. The interface should be so easy to navigate that the learning curve is minimal. An example is Apple's 'swipe' interaction on the iPhone or iPad. Once the screen is unlocked by using one finger, users have the model for all other interactions on that interface.

8   *Reduce any overload*
Don't have too many windows opening or too many tabs/options for users to navigate through or use. If elements are required, they should be added over time as users become more comfortable and experienced with the interface. Complexity should be added over time whenever possible.

4.2

4.2 **Web page error //
Specialmoves**

Design needs to be detail oriented and thoroughly thought through. Even an error message, such as 'page not found', must be useful and reflect the brand identity.

'Simplicity before understanding is simplistic; simplicity after understanding is simple.'

Edward De Bono, physician, author, inventor and design consultant

Magic Number Seven, Plus or Minus Two principle

The 'Magic Number Seven, Plus or Minus Two' principle comes from a 1956 psychological study by George A. Miller. He found that short-term memory works best when it uses 'chunks' of seven (plus or minus two) bits of data. Any more than that and the chances are people forget the options they've been given. Therefore, if users are given too many options in a navigation menu it's confusing and unusable.

The three-click rule

All content should be within easy reach of the user. This rule is often associated with the creators of the Palm PDA. This system was designed so that users could access any information they needed within three clicks. This rule underlines the need for clear, concise and streamlined interactions.

The two-second rule

If a user waits more than two seconds for some kind of response from an online application, they may assume it's not working or become bored and impatient. This does not mean that the application has to be super fast; instead, the application should always feedback to the user, for example using a 'now loading' animation.

These rules offer an insight into some of the approaches to usability a designer should consider. In any interactive project, it's vitally important to consider how the consumers will actually 'use' the product.

4.3

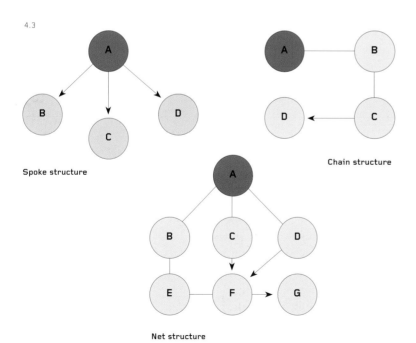

Spoke structure

Chain structure

Net structure

4.3 Navigation structures

There are several approaches to designing any information flow for an app or a website. Choices depend on the amount of content and the type of content. A spoke-hub structure is simple for sites such as portfolios. A chain structure is good for content that is more linear such as news. A net structure is more complex for sites such as Amazon.com, which has many sections and sub-sections.

Dieter Rams: ten principles for good design

Good design is innovative: The possibilities for innovation are not, by any means, exhausted. Technological development is always offering new opportunities for innovative design. But innovative design always develops in tandem with innovative technology, and can never be an end in itself.

Good design makes a product useful: A product is bought to be used. It has to satisfy certain criteria, not only functional but also psychological and aesthetic. Good design emphasizes the usefulness of a product whilst disregarding anything that could possibly detract from it.

Good design is aesthetic: The aesthetic quality of a product is integral to its usefulness because products we use every day affect our person and our well-being. But only well-executed objects can be beautiful.

Good design makes a product understandable: It clarifies the product's structure. Better still, it can make the product talk. At best, it is self-explanatory.

Good design is unobtrusive: Products fulfilling a purpose are like tools. They are neither decorative objects nor works of art. Their design should therefore be both neutral and restrained, to leave room for the user's self-expression.

Good design is honest: It does not make a product more innovative, powerful or valuable than it really is. It does not attempt to manipulate the consumer with promises that cannot be kept.

Good design is long-lasting: It avoids being fashionable and therefore never appears antiquated. Unlike fashionable design, it lasts many years – even in today's throwaway society.

Good design is thorough down to the last detail: Nothing must be arbitrary or left to chance. Care and accuracy in the design process show respect towards the user.

Good design is environmentally friendly: Design makes an important contribution to the preservation of the environment. It conserves resources and minimizes physical and visual pollution throughout the life cycle of the product.

Good design is as little design as possible: Less, but better – because it concentrates on the essential aspects, and the products are not burdened with non-essentials.

Back to purity, back to simplicity.

4.4 **Dieter Rams**

In the 1970s the legendary German industrial designer Dieter Rams asked himself if his design was 'good enough'. As a response he created ten principles for good design, which have since become fundamental to designers across disciplines.

4.4

Usability and content

There are usability methods that consider how people read, interact, share and engage with content. Given that so many people have less time to spend on so many aspects of their lives, usability focuses on enabling the most rewarding experience as quickly as possible, while also allowing for deeper content to be delivered if desired. These are some principles to consider when developing the layout and content for an interactive project.

The inverted pyramid
The inverted pyramid is a writing style used by news sites that works across much text-based media; it's also known as the 'Waterfall Effect'. For example, a newspaper will have a headline and short summary (subtitle) of the contents of the story that invites the reader into the article. The article will begin with a 'conclusion', then offers key points and background information. The inverted pyramid system draws a reader into a larger article in small, easy to digest chunks.

4.5 The waterfall effect

Look at any newspaper or web-based news and you will see the waterfall effect in action.

4.5

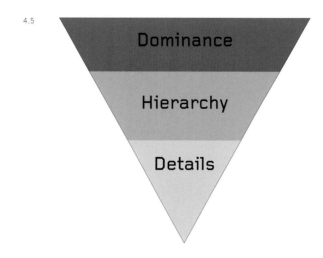

98

Baby duck syndrome

Baby duck syndrome is a tendency for users to 'imprint' on the design they first encounter and then stick with it. This is best exemplified when a website or application is redesigned (e.g. the furore when Facebook changed their site design). People are resistant to change and love the familiar; they tend to judge other designs or systems based on what they already know, so users of the Apple OS may extol its virtues (what they know) against all that is 'wrong' with the Windows OS (the unfamiliar). When redesigning a site or application the designer must consider the reactions of the user-base and try to find ways to limit backlash (an easier to use interface or introducing changes in smaller increments).

The Zeigarnik effect

The Zeigarnik effect, also known as the 'cliffhanger effect', is used in media as a form of marketing. Bluma Zeigarnik was a Russian psychologist who found that people are more likely to remember something that is unfinished or incomplete. For example, at the end of an episode of a crime drama there is often a scene that encourages people to tune-in next week to find out what happens. This tactic is employed to drive users around an app or a website, as well as invite them to come back. For example, offering RSS feeds (Real Simple Syndication is a text-based notification that can be delivered from a website via email or other applications) gives a very quick summary of new content appearing on a website. Updates to an iPhone app can drive users back to the product. It can be subtle; when an article is finished, it could offer links to similar articles by that author or to similar subject matter – all driving customers to access more of the site content.

The self-reference effect

The self-reference effect dramatically improves the communication between author and audience, and helps with information retention (if users remember a site and an article they are more likely to share the article or return to the site later). The best examples of this effect are the comments or feedback areas on a site. It connects the user with a community and often the writer. Once users are involved they are much more inclined to revisit the site.

'The more users' expectations prove right, the more they will feel in control of the system and the more they will like it.'

Jakob Nielsen, web-usability consultant

Usability and visual communication

This section further explores the principles of how an audience perceives content and the guidelines covering the psychology of usability. Designers may assume audiences look at the art assets on a website and then click the button designed to be pressed, but this is not always the case; designers need to be aware and understand how people actually use a product.

Eyeline

Knowing where users are looking on a page or screen is a useful way of directing them towards important content. Faces are a great way of doing this; humans are always attracted to looking at faces. What's interesting is that once users have locked onto a face, they tend to look in the same direction as the person in that image. If a designer wants to attract users to a certain area of the page (an advert, image or headline) this principle can work well.

4.7

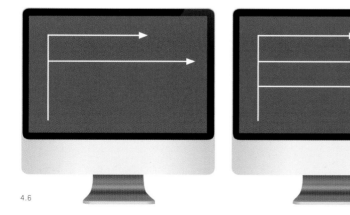

4.6

4.6–4.7 Eye-tracking experiments

In 1970, Swiss psychologist Hans-Werner Hunziker created one of the earliest tests to track eye movements while people were problem solving. Filmed through a plate of glass, Hunziker was able to track the eye's movements as a problem was solved, giving him insight into eye movement, attention and the thought process.

4.8

4.8 **The rule of odds**

Surrounding an object of interest with an odd number of other objects is pleasing to the eye.

Good design credibility

People are more likely to engage with a well-designed site because a good-looking site equates to credibility in the mind of consumers. People learn that good designs (products and images that look good and are well made) are more expensive than badly designed or shoddy products. This translates to media and websites. If the site looks good and relates well to the intended audience, people will instinctively trust the site and worry less about buying from the site. A simple spelling mistake or bad grammar (along with bland images) can be enough to make the site seem untrustworthy.

Don't be afraid of white space

As with a visual composition, white space is important. When used wisely, it allows users time to look around the space without being bombarded with images and text. Visual clutter is very damaging, and projects that cram too much into their first screen have a slightly desperate feel to them. The white space doesn't have to be white, it can be the background colour or space in-between paragraphs.

Rule of odds

As in the image above, the rule of odds creates interest or focus for any image or content that is surrounded by an uneven number of other content. Three is better than two or four in a composition, people find it more visually agreeable.

Symmetry/asymmetry

Symmetry in design can be achieved by placing like objects side by side to achieve balance and form. For example, four identical white vases on a shelf. Asymmetry disrupts this format and can draw the eye directly to an intended object. For example what if the third vase was much smaller and bright blue?

101

Usability testing

As we saw in chapter 2, prototyping and sketching enhance the smoothness of the development process. This principle is crucial to provide insights into any problems related to the layout or interactivity design. Testing those prototypes and relating that feedback into the next prototype is an important part of the usability process.

TETO: Test Early, Test Often
Steve Krug, in his book on web usability *Don't Make Me Think*, outlines some important elements on testing interactive designs.

1   *'If you want a great site, you've got to test'*
    Any team or designer who has been working on a project for a few weeks will never be able to approach the project with 'fresh eyes'. Showing it to other people to test is a great way of getting quick feedback.

2   *'Testing one user is 100 per cent better than testing none'*
    Any form of testing works to improve the project. As we see in the case study, Future Platforms (page 106) didn't have time to get users in from outside so they tested their app on other people in the studio, family and friends. Often that's enough to get relevant and useful feedback.

3   *'Testing one user early in the project is better than testing 50 near the end'*
    If a designer tests early enough, testing never becomes a big deal that can take up too much time. If anything, testing the prototypes and smaller versions of a larger project is more useful because it's instantaneous.

4   *'Testing is an iterative process'*
    It's not something a designer will do once and then assume it's all just going to fall into place from there on. Every project manager will have testing cycles built into the timeframe of a project. Even so, it is a good idea to ask other people in the studio to look over a new feature.

4.9

4.10

4.9–4.10
Testing and iteration

Technical projects have to be
tested by the team early on,
and by other neutral parties
closer to the launch. Testing
is not just to find the broken
parts. When done properly
it can highlight areas that are
particularly successful and gives
the team an idea of where to
focus their efforts.

Interview: Trevor May, mobile designer

Trevor May specializes in interactive mobile design. He is the senior designer at Ribot in Brighton, UK, and previously worked at Future Platforms, UK.

What do you see as the differences between designing for mobile over other media platforms (web/desktop, home/office use)?

Mobile applications (apps) tend to be more task focused. That's not to say other media shouldn't be, but it's even more important when you're creating interactivity for a small-screen device and an 'on-the-go' user. The mobile user does not have the luxury of time and contemplation. For mobile, you'll need to consider carefully how easy it is for the user to find important information or perform a specific task; and then design those priorities into the interactive experience.

When a designer is adapting content that's used on the Web it's worth asking what content is necessary, and then consider dropping functionality or information that's non-essential. For example, compare the desktop versions of Amazon, YouTube and eBay to their mobile app counterparts to see how less important content is removed or presented lower down the 'stack' (the stack refers in part to the 'three-click' rule, it's layers of information or content that are stacked with the most relevant and important being on 'top').

Do you feel that experiences are different with mobile compared to other media formats?

The main issue is that pixel density is much greater on mobile devices (and the screens are a lot smaller); so while elements of a layout may appear generously spaced on a low-density laptop screen, they may be fiddly on a mobile's screen. It's very important to test designs on the device on which they will be delivered – even if they're static mock-ups – to get a better idea of whether they're going to work.

What are some of the traps or pitfalls to avoid with mobile development?

Different mobile operating systems have different conventions that the user would already be familiar with. A common mistake is to directly post an app from one platform, like iOS (Apple), to another, like Android, leaving in navigation elements which are inappropriate, such as the back button.

Android and Windows phones include a physical or 'hard' back button that acts in a similar way to the back button of a web browser or Windows Explorer. The user expects it to work in this way on those platforms and often a user's forward/backward flow can easily be broken without proper testing. iOS offers the user a bit more control as it relies on the developer providing a 'soft' back button, however it's important to remain consistent to each platform.

If someone was getting into designing specifically for mobile, what would be your advice?

The first step would be to get a variety of different handsets and use them as your 'main' phone. Learn their differences, quirks and similarities. Study how the apps work and analyse how the same app works across different phones (for example, what are the differences between IMDB.com on an Android device compared to the iPhone? The differences might be subtle, but important). Study how websites work too, in particular the flow of navigation and content delivery. To practice, find a website or desktop app and figure out how you'd adapt it to work on a mobile device.

Do you see concentrating on mobile as a large part of the future, or a niche area?

Mobile is a big part of the picture. As we're becoming more 'always on', we ultimately expect more from our digital services, whether they be on mobile or elsewhere. We expect them to be integrated. If I start an order on my phone, I want to be able to pick up my basket and carry it onto a desktop, seamlessly. I expect to be able to set my TiVo to record a TV show from my iPhone while I'm on vacation. In that sense, the mobile is becoming an essential part of any digital service.

In the years you've been working on mobile apps, what has changed the most?

It's a technology that's constantly changing and evolving. Even in just the last couple of years we've seen a massive shift of use from the traditional 'feature phones' to so-called smartphones, Android, iPhones and now the Windows Phone. The biggest change has been in the quality of the screen and we've seen huge leaps in processing power in these devices. The main aspect of designing for mobile over desktop hasn't really changed; as the technology advances and devices become faster and more powerful, it's always the case that users expect more from the software that runs on it. Our job is to make the interfaces and content on these devices as positive an experience as possible.

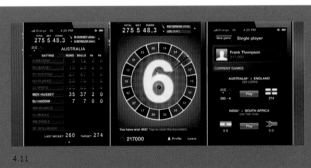

4.11

4.12

4.13

4.11–4.13 **Design for mobile**

Designing for mobile isn't the same as designing for the computer. It's not just about screen size but also understanding how and where people use mobile content. Increasingly, mobile is where people access content the most. Shown are a series of apps created while Trevor was at Future Platforms.

Case study:
Glastonbury app

Studio: Future Platforms, UK
Client: Orange Communications

Future Platforms are a small studio based in Brighton, UK. They make 'lovely things for mobile phones', for companies such as Nokia, Orange, the BBC and lastminute.com. They won the pitch to create a smartphone app for the largest music festival in the world – the Glastonbury Music Festival. The app needed to run on iOS, Android and Nokia platforms.

Winning the pitch

Ideas and innovation won Future Platforms the pitch for the Glastonbury app. The team examined the elements of what people would expect from a festival app and then developed concepts far beyond those expectations and created a truly innovative and inclusive application for music fans.

The concept was straightforward; the team knew that there were a set of elements that people would expect from a Glastonbury app, such as up-to-date listings and a site map. So it was important to produce those well. Artist line-ups are always printed and handed out at the site entry, but they're frequently revised up to the last minute; therefore, an app needed to include these live updates too. As festival tickets sell out quickly, there is a large Glastonbury audience that only experience it through TV, music press, or late-night texts from friends, so that audience also had to be considered.

Challenges and audience considerations

Many of the team had been to the Glastonbury festival, so usefully the office test audience had local knowledge.

The challenge was to consider battery life: minimizing use of the network (battery drain); prioritizing how the app would be used most and connecting people. The team decided that the key features of the app would be:

- A great looking Electronic Programme Guide (EPG) that grabs line-ups (and changes) efficiently, stores them on a phone and allows ease of selection.
- A personal itinerary – users fill in their favourite acts, and alarms alert them when the acts are on.
- Full site maps showing where the user is.
- Easy sharing of events through Facebook, so that users could tell everyone at home exactly what they're missing.
- A live 'heat map' telling users where the hottest action is. The map data was gathered from 'mood data' mined from the app and users uploading information to Facebook. An interesting experiment in crowd dynamics that enabled users to track where people were, and what made an area 'hot' or 'cold' based on what was happening at the festival.
- A news section, which Orange would update before and during the event.

Art direction and design

When it came to visuals and aesthetics the team had a head start; the Orange and *The Guardian* (a UK-based newspaper) brands were natural bedfellows, so much of the colour scheme, look and feel were influenced by the brands. The team focused on giving the app the Orange 'feel'.

The icon is a chromatic microcosm of the app (clean and simple) and *The Guardian's* rainbow icon supplied the colour-scheme for the app. Dark colours and a black background were used simply because OLED screens use much less power when displaying black.

4.14 Glastonbury Festival app // Future Platforms

The Glastonbury Festival app mock-up as it appears on an iPhone – specific care has been taken with the art direction to allow the brand recognition of Orange and the *The Guardian* newspaper to come through.

Future Platforms spent a lot of time creating the map. They used high-contrast stage names that have a subtle stroke around the labels to maintain legibility on a small screen. Research into **wayfinding** also informed the look and feel of the map, inspired by everyday signage.

schedule

map

news

about

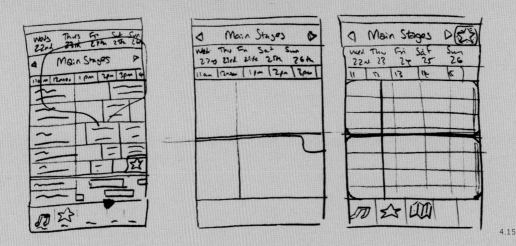

4.15

4.15 Mobile wireframes

Early interactive wireframes illustrate some of the
navigation and interaction elements proposed for the app.

4.16 The final app

Designing for the small screen is not easy – the content has to work
at a glance and on closer inspection. Using a contrasting, bold colour
scheme, as well as icons, helps communicate the usability of the app.

Prototyping the project

The centre of the app is the Electronic Programme
Guide (EPG). In early workshops, the Clashfinder
service was mentioned as being popular (Clashfinder
is a free, printable timetable to a music festival or other
event), primarily because of its personalized nature.

Therefore, these, and the interfaces for recording
devices, were inspirations for the EPG. It was sketched
and prototyped very early on. The high-definition
prototype (built in HTML and CSS) was particularly
useful to explain the workings of the EPG to Orange,
and acted as a reference for the developers.

The technology

The normal way to go cross-platform is by using
HTML5 and web technologies, but experimentation
proved these inappropriate. High-performance user
interfaces, large offline storage and deep integration
with handset features were required.

Glastonbury 2011 is the first product launched
publicly to pioneer a new approach – of combining
mobile web features with native application features
to create a seamless and slick hybrid.

PROJECT TOOLS

- Software – iOS: Xcode, Android/Qt: Eclipse
- Hardware – A combination of Macs running OS X
  (essential for iOS development) and Windows 7 PCs

4.16

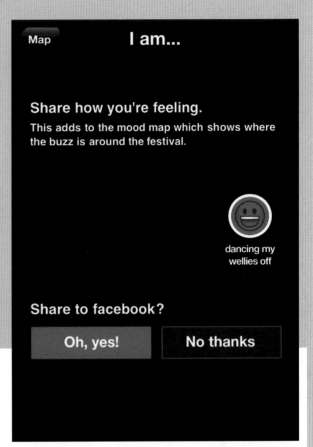

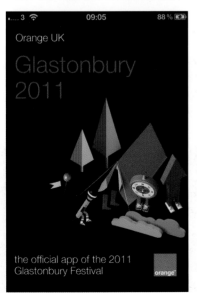

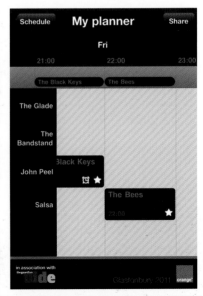

Project:
Create an interactive promotion

The brief

Create an in-store interactive promotion for a sportswear brand such as Umbro (a middle-brand sportswear label). The promotion is aimed at the 14–25 year old male and female market. The brief is to connect the brand with the youth demographic in the Americas and Europe in an innovative and engaging way, using social media, rich media and interactive artefacts. The project can focus on one product, a range of sportswear or the entire store.

1 Research and sketching

Working individually or in teams, research the current successful and non-successful approaches to in-store promotions. This will involve going to stores/shops in malls and physical locations to see what Umbro and its peer brands are currently doing. Who do Umbro sponsor? Who should they be sponsoring?

(a) Create four personas, two male and two female, who fit within this demographic.

(b) Create and document three mock-up/sketch ideas from your research of possible in-store promotions.

Considerations

■ What would persuade people of that demographic into a store and to interact with the product?

■ Would using athletes raise brand or product awareness? If so, from which sport?

■ Is the project limited to an in-store experience only? Would it or could it live on in other media (e.g. apps, website or print)? How would those media be integrated?

2 Prototype

Based on feedback from other team members choose one project idea to move forward with.

Create a detailed image-rich multimedia presentation (use PowerPoint, Flash Catalyst, video/animation) of the concept basing it on your research, innovation, imagination and the personas you created. As part of the presentation, use the personas to create a scenario in storyboard or comic-book format to take each persona through the experience of using the in-store promotion. Make sure the audience for your presentation understand how the interaction works (e.g. navigation, manipulation, usability and instructions), and how the personas would engage with your concept.

Considerations

■ What delivery platform will work? Mobile, tablet, smartphone? Should it be proprietary and built specifically for flagship stores?

■ What forms of alternative technologies could be used? Movement sensors that trigger video or interactive audio, for example? Game consoles? Touch screens?

■ How could the experience drive sales or product awareness?

Tips!

1 Don't assume a 'like' or a 'tweet' will mean increased sales!

2 Prototypes must consider the platform.

3 Stay focused on the brand identity.

4 Don't use technology just for technology's sake.

5.1

Chapter 5: Motion Graphics and Shareable Media

5.1 **Wrangler Blue Bell // Kokokaka**

Kokokaka employed interactive video for the Wrangler Blue Bell campaign. The models wearing the Blue Bell range could be manipulated within the video environment (dressed/undressed) to great effect.

Motion and interactivity

'Creativity is magical, but is not magic.'

Charles Limb, musical creator

It's useful for interactive designers to know about the basics of **motion graphics** and video production. A video can be interactive and social; if it's engaging to an audience, it can advertise or extend a project. Adopting the right strategy across mediums, such as YouTube and social media, is part of the **lexicon** of interactive design.

Advertising campaigns, products and educational projects are all launched in multiple ways across multiple media platforms. A website may call for video to be part of the content as well as an interactive game, ad banner or application. The world of the interactive designer is the world of YouTube, Vimeo, video games, the Web and, increasingly, TV.

Being an animator, motion designer or video production designer is a speciality in itself. Interactive designers are not expected to have in-depth knowledge of the intricacies of these production processes. They should have enough knowledge of, and be comfortable with, video production/shooting and editing, animation or motion (using programs such as Apple's Final Cut Studio and Adobe After Effects), and be able to produce work that can give a sense of the vision for a project.

Interactive video
Video used to be a passive experience, something people just watched. Audiences increasingly expect more from their media. Michael Lebowitz, the CEO and founder of Big Spaceship (NYC), sums up the new relationship with marketing within the new media space, 'We're not trying to persuade people of things anymore, what we're doing is earning their attention by giving more than we expect in return.' The ability to interact, create, share and remix video content adds an additional layer of depth to an experience and can lead to larger page views and increased awareness of the product, which is what the client always wants.

5.2

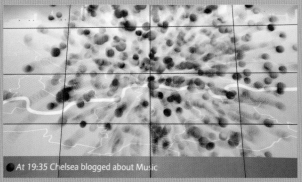

At 19:35 Chelsea blogged about Music

5.3

5.2–5.3 **Barclays // The One Off**

The One Off (UK) created an installation for Barclays Bank in Piccadilly, London (UK) that goes beyond advertising just the bank's services and information. The concept was to create a warm, engaging interactive experience for visitors. The large-format screen 'scrapes' data feeds from a variety of sources and then generates graphics depicting the current 'mood' of London, as well as live events and tourist-related information. The data is responsive to the time and weather as well as the input of users and 'intelligently' alters its feedback based on a variety of factors.

Every interaction with the Barclays' giant screen launches a colourful animation, with each colour representing a different cultural event.

5.4

5.5

5.4–5.8 Adler Planetarium // Second Story and Snibbe Interactive

The challenge for this project created by Second Story and Snibbe Interactive (US) was to create an interactive animated experience for the Adler Planetarium (Chicago, US) that would communicate space exploration and answer some of the big questions of science.

The environment used an interactive projection that filled four walls of the gallery. The shadows of visitors become reactive as their silhouettes control and manipulate objects on the walls of the gallery or interact with questions and facts.

Levels of engagement are greater when the audience can play with the exhibition. The visitor is engaged in the content because they are immersed in it through their own movement.

5.6

5.7

5.8

Multiple media projects

Multiple media projects, such as the Wrangler Blue Bell campaign (see images 5.9–5.11), are usually created in teams that include interactive designers, writers, artists, animators and video production people. The role of interactive designers is to examine and plan how the interaction can enrich the project outcomes. Although assets may be created by other art and media teams, it is the job of interactive designers to bring it all together into a cohesive final project, seamlessly integrating the media into an engaging interactive experience that gives the audience something new.

Interactive online videos are true multimedia projects, realized through the application of many technologies. It's one thing to watch a model wearing clothes, it's a more rewarding experience to be able to alter or play with the environment of that character and influence the narrative.

Immersive experiences, such as those created by Second Story for the Adler Planetarium in Chicago (see images 5.4–5.8 on pages 116–7), combine animation, photography, video, interactive walls and reactive shadows. This exhibition experience requires the physical participation of the visitors to fully interact with the assets to complete the immersive experience.

5.9–5.11 Wrangler Blue Bell // Kokokaka

Kokokaka created an interactive video experience for the Wrangler Blue Bell campaign. The user can interact with the model. As the user drags the mouse left or right the model has his clothes ripped off. Individual frames from the video can be shared via social media sites to draw attention to the campaign.

5.9

5.10

5.11

Animatics and video prototypes

Video and animation can be employed by interactive design teams during the prototyping phase to persuade a client or audience of the aesthetics and art direction of a project. It's sometimes quicker to create an **animatic** or previsualization of a large project or application instead of spending time programming when the team's aim is to give the client a sense of their overall vision.

When creating a proof of concept, an animated video can take a viewer through the concepts and controlled interactions of a solution before the team commits to building the interactive prototypes. Animations (usually produced by animators and motion designers) often include a soundtrack and a walk through of the project's intended purpose, which helps to communicate the team's ideas. The video or animation can be thought of as a trailer for the project, right down to the inclusion of voice-overs, music and any other media that communicates the aesthetic and intention of the initial proposal. Most design agencies have motion designers and animators on staff, but if the studio is small it may become the job of the graphic and interaction designer to put together the presentation. This is where some knowledge of the tools of video and animation can be useful.

5.12

5.13

5.12–5.13 **Sky Broadcast // The One Off**

The One Off developed a touch screen for the UK's Sky Broadcast stores. The concept was to create an intuitive installation that would encourage customers to sign up for TV packages. The animations and gestures mimic those people are used to seeing on tablet devices and smartphones. So although this is a large screen, it was designed to work and look familiar to most customers.

5.14

5.16

5.15

5.14–5.16 **University of Oregon Ford Alumni Center // Second Story**

A series of media installations create an engaging and inspiring entrance way at the University of Oregon, US. Looking to engage the audience with an immersive experience, Second Story created a dynamic series of touch screens, video walls and LED walls that display a variety of rich media.

Another set of tools

Some of the tools used by interactive designers are also used by motion and video production teams. For example, Adobe Flash was originally designed as an animation tool. Photoshop and Illustrator are core art producers. Images created with these applications can be integrated into video and animation packages (Adobe and Apple both have their own video-editing suites).

Shooting video, editing and adding visual effects have become easier with tools such as Apple's Final Cut Studio and Adobe's post-production tool, After Effects, which is also used for compositing, visual effects and in post-production – it can even be used for animation. In short, After Effects is Photoshop for video.

It is important that interactive designers understand the place and possibilities of animation and video within the interactive media space. For example, Nike's 'Quick Control Chaos' <www.nike.com/jumpman23/cp3v/chaos> has multiple layers of interactive video, enabling the user to control time and the camera angle. Interactive video is becoming more popular as high-bandwidth Internet becomes more accessible.

Julian Oliver's *levelHead* is a project that integrates animation, video and augmented reality (AR) into a new form of interactive game.

5.17–5.18 levelHead // Julian Oliver

levelHead is a spatial memory game created by Julian Oliver (a New Zealander working in Germany). It is controlled by a game interface with a solid plastic cube with augmented reality markers on it. When viewed on-screen the AR replaces the cube's surfaces with an animation of empty rooms. The physical manipulation of the cube acts as a controller for completing the game. By tilting the cube, the player controls a character's movement and has to direct it towards an exit. There are three cubes (or levels) which are connected; players have to find the final exit door by manipulating the environment, not the game character.

5.17

5.18

Augmented reality

Augmented reality (AR) uses a camera feed (such as a web cam or phone cam) and overlays media onto the live visuals. AR is being used by designers to inform and entertain by adding layers of images and data to a live view.

An augmented street view application (such as Localscope by Cynapse) uses a phone's GPS coordinates (the phone knows where you are) and the accelerometer (the phone knows where you are looking) to overlay reviews of restaurants in real time when the user holds the phone up and points it towards a row of restaurants.

The UK-based Appshaker studio created an augmented reality experience for the National Geographic Channel in a mall in Hungary. The AR application used printed cards with trackers (small barcode-like images) on them to register the user's position. The AR then projected an image to match where users were on-screen. When the audience saw themselves on a large screen in the mall, they were surrounded by dinosaurs, leopards or dolphins in real time. It's similar to live green-screen effects, such as those used by weather presenters; the difference is that AR can be manipulated by the users.

AR objects can be 'held', kicked or played with, deepening the level of immersion and interaction. Development with trackerless AR software has meant that more interactive projects can be created that work with many people in an audience, not just those who have access to a printed tracker image.

5.19–5.23 National Geographic Channel // Appshaker

This augmented reality project created by Appshaker (UK) took place in a mall as part of a campaign for the National Geographic Channel. When standing in the correct space the audience would see themselves surrounded by animated dinosaurs or wild animals, which were projected live into the shoppers' environment. The integration of the creatures and the audience interactions were projected onto a large video screen in the mall.

'Virtual reality promises a kind of transcendence of the limits of physical reality.'

Frank Biocca, Taeyong Kim and Mark R. Levy, *Communication in the Age of Virtual Reality*

5.19

5.20

5.21

5.22

5.24

5.24–5.27 National Geographic Channel // Appshaker

The National Geographic logo was a large AR marker which enabled the software to know the location of the audience. Markers were also printed on hand-held postcards which enabled live intimate experiences to occur between the audience and the animated content. The installation also incorporated audio specific to each animation adding another layer of believability and immersion to the experience.

5.25

5.26

5.27

Video and motion graphics

When thinking about how to integrate video or animation into a project, it's useful to know some of the fundamentals of the production process. It is important for designers to be able to create assets suitable for the output media, as well as to understand the possibilities of the medium, so that they can create a more rewarding or deeper experience for the audience.

Motion graphics

Motion graphics are defined separately from animation because they are often created to inform or to enhance a video rather than be a part of a narrative structure. An introductory video that pulls the audience into the themes and 'brand environment' is a useful tool, and the kinetic nature of motion graphics is immediately engaging. Video and animation are often employed to drive a narrative for a brand, as for some audiences it's easier than having to click through multiple screens to get the same information.

5.28–5.30 Samsung immersive animation // Studio La Flama

For the launch of Samsung's Smart TV, Studio La Flama created a series of animations and motion graphics to enhance the live launch event. The audience were surrounded by projections of the animations, which seemed to explode out of a 3D box into the environment creating an engaging and immersive experience.

5.28

5.29

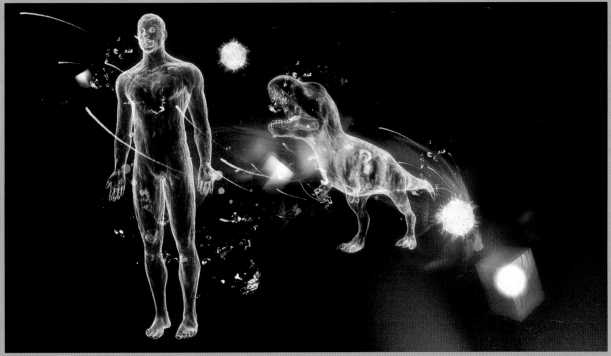

5.30

5.31

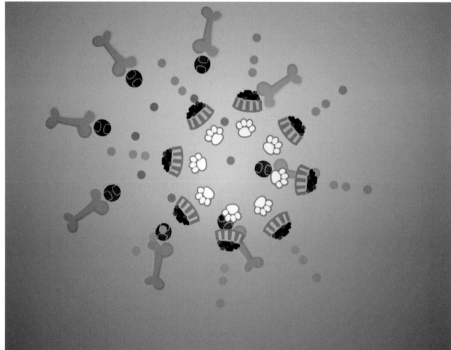

5.31–5.33 Pet of the month // Krystal Schultheiss

This title sequence was put together by Krystal Schultheiss (Australia) to introduce the March 2011 Pet of the Month short video for the Upmarket Pets online community. As part of the campaign, a new video was available online every month to engage the company with their online customer base and community. The animations were bright, colourful and fun in order to connect with as broad an audience as possible.

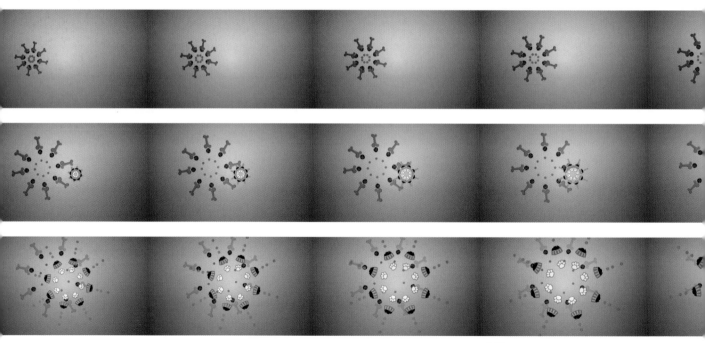

5.33

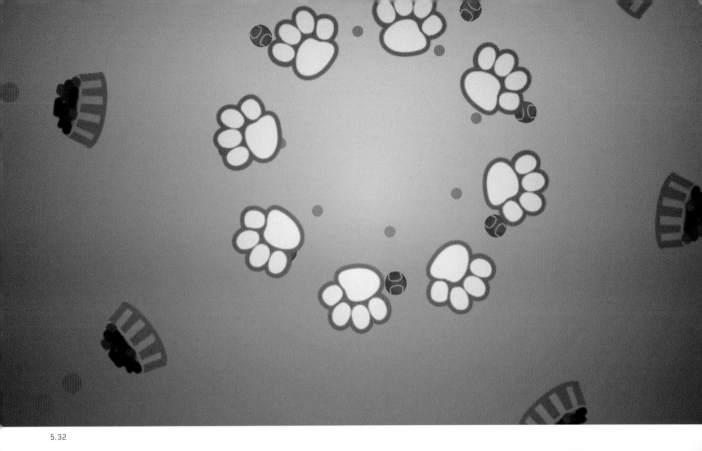

5.32

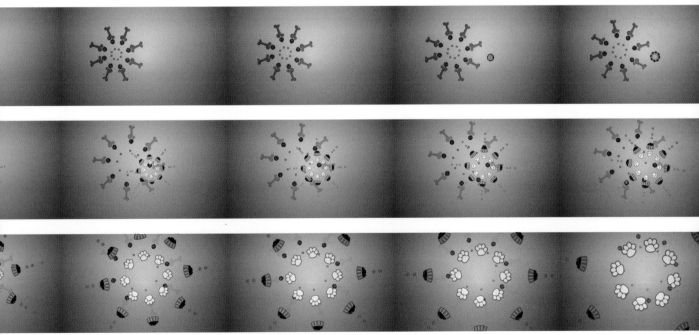

Interview: Krystal Schultheiss, motion graphics designer

As a motion graphics designer at Caramel Creative in Melbourne, Australia, Krystal has worked on a diverse range of projects and platforms from broadcast to the Web and mobile.

What are motion graphics?

Motion graphics are graphics that move. The source of the graphics can range from video, photography to typography, graphic design and illustration. The focus of motion graphics is to edit the timing and movement of the graphics, which is as important as the design of the graphics. Timing and motion can add character to even the simplest of geometric shapes.

What are the fundamental skills motion graphic designers require?

The minimum is knowledge of traditional 2D-animation skills and an understanding of the language of film.

Traditional animation skills help motion designers know how to plan a motion graphics project. The planning of a project is essential before using animation computer software. Motion designers are effectively a hybrid of animator and video editor, they must understand traditional animation fundamentals such as 'keyframing', 'in-betweening' and 'exaggeration' and, as editors, be able to set the tone and pace of a project.

Traditional design skills and 3D-software skills also help motion graphics artists fulfil their role. Knowing design fundamentals such as typography, layout and colour theory increases aesthetic impact and helps to communicate to an audience. Knowledge of 3D software and its workflow can assist motion graphics designers in creating efficient 2D and 3D environments.

What is the production process for creating a motion project from a brief?

A motion graphics work always starts as a script, storyboard and then an animatic before it enters a production phase. A script can be a brief list of intentions in answer to a problem, or it can be a very detailed script. Once an idea or story is created, it is best to break it down visually with a storyboard. The storyboard contains every visual keyframe and exaggeration. It may also have action, camera and studio descriptions of each frame. From here, a storyboard is then turned into an animatic, a simple animation or motion video where each keyframe and exaggeration are synced to audio in a movie file.

What is the process for incorporating motion artwork into an interactive project? At what point are you involved?

Every interactive project is different and requires careful planning by an experienced art director. As interactive projects are non-linear in nature, they require collaboration with the design team and the skill sets of an interactive designer or builder (coder).

Whom do you work with most closely on a project?

I work closely with the strategic director and the creative director. I work with them in the planning phases to most effectively communicate the message visually. On some projects, I am the art director and have that level of control and input, whereas on others I design the video along with ideas and guidance from my creative director. When I am art directing a project, I usually work with a strategic director who creates the script and overall focus of the project to give me something to work from.

What tools do you normally use on a project?

It usually starts with pen and paper and a dot grid sketchbook. I also use Adobe Illustrator, Adobe After Effects, Photoshop and Cinema 4D.

How does the delivery platform affect the motion graphic design (e.g. web to mobile)?

The main concern for motion graphics designers is the Web. Internet browsers on personal computers and mobile platforms vary immensely in the types of video format they can play. Motion designers need to know about compression and video formats in order to publish work online. Before starting any motion graphics project, designers must investigate where the project will be viewed and design according to that space or multiple-delivery platforms.

What other areas should be considered when thinking about motion design?

You must learn about traditional design elements and principles. Learn to storyboard your motion projects – it saves time and money when working with clients. Learn about both 2D and 3D animation. Also learn about sound and music. Audio makes up 80 per cent of any motion graphics project – it adds depth and it is a critical element of communication.

5.34 'Smash the Planet' title sequence for the 'unEarth' television series // Krystal Schultheiss

Motion graphics are used to convey meaning and aesthetic resonance composited in with other visuals. In many cases motion graphics are the animated title sequence of a program, **ident** or film. They are critically important because they convey, encapsulate and advertise the feature's content.

5.34

The video production process

Shooting digital video is not hard, the issues come in thinking in motion/time-based media and realizing how much experience goes into being good at video production. If this is the case, you need to call in the experts. Even so, solid results can be achieved with a good video camera, some knowledge of video editing software and an action plan.

The general rule for video is: plan the shoot, shoot the plan. Video is an instant medium, anyone can grab a camera hit the record button and start shooting. The more professional process has to be driven by an idea, an aesthetic and ultimately, a plan of action. Going from idea to final edited video is usually referred to as a 'workflow'. The workflow has to take into account every aspect of the process from those initial sketches to any art assets, location scouting and shooting, permissions, actors, scripts, animations or titles, sound/audio, editing, visual effects and post-production. Even for small productions and student projects there are fundamental workflow steps that, when followed, ensure the video-production process goes smoothly.

5.35

5.35–5.37 Social Studio // Krystal Schultheiss

In this TV commercial for The Social Studio TVC in Melbourne, Australia, the video footage is shot and edited and then motion graphics are overlaid to add a dynamic and kinetic aesthetic. The graphics, which include the logo and taglines of the organization, add depth and a richer sense of visual design to the commercial.

Pre-production and shooting

1   *Concept creation:* as with any design solution the project has to be idea driven. When creating concepts the team has to bear in mind not only what is possible and required by the client, but also what is affordable on the budget.

2   *Scriptwriting:* even if there's no dialogue or spoken word required for the video, a script can touch on the mood and feeling and guide the shoot. The script helps the shooting and editing teams hit the 'beats' of the production in time with the desired moments of visual impact or importance.

3   *Production planning (pre-production):* storyboards and previsualizations are created once the concept and script are finalized. Storyboards plan and visualize the camera positioning, movement and action elements. They can be detailed or more of an overview.

4   *Videography (shoot):* this can be the expensive part as potentially a production could include actors, directors, film crew, audio people, lighting, camera operators, artists, stylists, catering and so on. This is why having a plan and a storyboard allows everyone to know what's going on and streamlines the process.

5   *Graphic asset creation and design:* when shooting for a corporate client there may be assets that have to be included, such as a client's logo, certain colouration, or art assets that coordinate with other campaigns and media (e.g. the website and print ads). This should run in parallel to the production planning as it can be time-consuming to create these assets.

6   *Voice-over (VO):* voice talent is cheaper than acted dialogue, so a VO could dispense with actors. It may be that the concept calls for a VO to set a scene or to voice the tagline at the end of a video.

7   *Music, soundtracks and audio effects:* does the production call for an original score? If so, the music needs to be composed; if not, then rights need to be attained for any popular song that is used in the production. Creating or choosing the right music for the aesthetic and emotion of the video is crucial. This can involve going against your personal choices and tastes. The team may all love a certain style of music, but is that going to work for the video?

5.36

5.37

Post-production

Post-production is the next step in the process. Once all assets have been created, video is shot and footage is ready to be prepared for final output. This is a vital part of the workflow and the design teams have to figure the post-production process into the project management.

1 *Editing (post-production):* the initial edit will be a 'rough cut' that has the footage matched up roughly to the soundtrack and/or voice-over that has been created. If the soundtrack is changed during the edit process, the editor may have to restart as the timing and feel of the production will suffer.

2 *Motion graphics and special effects:* at this point the art assets, which could be static or motion graphics, are brought in to layer over the video footage. This is where the video gets its polish and deeper aesthetic. Special effects can take a myriad of forms from mattes to super-imposed explosions, to a specific coloration and composition. Elements of motion graphics can also be composited in.

3 *The finalized edit, audio mix and master:* this is the finished project, everything has been composited together, all elements are mixed and then colour balanced (to make sure that each shot looks as good as it can and is consistent to the overall aesthetic). The audio and video are optimized for technical levels and standards (broadcast is very fussy about the colours you can use). The final edit is 'mastered' to the formats required for the project.

The production process can be deep and very intricate, but sometimes the entire process is incredibly short. It all depends on the budget and format the client wants. For example, viral videos are created quickly and often cheaply. The viral video's low-fidelity or amateur aesthetic is often an integral part of the authenticity desired by the marketing team. As with all design media, the level of quality is dependent on the campaign or product and is adjusted to suit the needs of the client.

'Art does not reproduce what we see; rather, it makes us see.'

Paul Klee, Swiss expressionist painter

5.38–5.42 HMV Live // Studio Output

This HMV Live ident was created by Studio Output in conjunction with Mainframe studio (animation) and SNK (audio) to promote the music store's live events. The focus on creating the short (six second) motion graphic was on communicating the energy, hipness and excitement of a live music event. The ident engages the audience as a visual 'burst' working with the music to introduce the content.

5.38

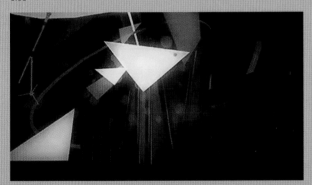

5.39

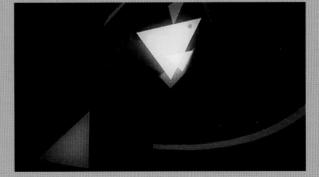

5.40

5.41

5.42

Viral videos

Online media space has opened up a new creative arena for advertising, marketing and cultural production. Websites such as YouTube and Vimeo allow people to create their own videos and share them with the world. This has mixed results, but some videos with incredibly low-production values and very amateur content have produced massive amounts of web traffic and have their own cult following.

There is a lot of competition for audiences' attention. So much video now competes directly with mainstream media advertising and brand campaigns that it's harder for products and services to be noticed. Agencies have embraced the popularity of sites like YouTube and realized that the online space has a different attention span and expectations to that of broadcast media. This, coupled with the power to share, has resulted in agencies creating the 'video viral' as part of an advertising campaign.

However, creating a video to go viral is not easy. Kevin Allocca, trends manager at YouTube, says that videos become viral because of three elements: 'Taste-makers, communities of participation and unexpectedness'.

Taste-makers are people in the media or well-connected bloggers who have large online audiences: once they tweet or tell others about the video it's very likely to get many hits.

Communities of participation are online communities that are likely to pass on the clip; these people could be colleagues or communities with shared online interests.

Unexpectedness is the hardest element to achieve, and it's the most elusive. Who would have thought a man halfway up a mountain commenting on a double rainbow would garner millions of hits, or that a badly animated cat scrolling across a screen endlessly would become a genuine phenomenon, with people remixing and remaking the video and posting versions of it back onto YouTube.

Using viral video

Virals – usually short, edgy and often funny – are designed for the short attention spans of online users with the knowledge that other content is only a click away. Creating successful virals has become big business and many of the amateur Internet video 'celebrities' have been snapped up by brands to advertise products; their purpose being to quickly tap into the cultural **zeitgeist**.

5.43–5.45 **Lynx Unleash the Chaos // Soap Creative**

The Unleash the Chaos campaign for Lynx was created in an unassuming house on a regular city street. The windows appear to be empty, but when passers-by put on special polarized glasses, they see the 'invisible' content. Different glasses revealed different content.

Virals are designed to have their content shared from one viewer to another to create a 'buzz' about a brand or product. As with cult movies, virals are hard to predict; some of the most amazing high-production virals garner few hits, whereas others strike the right note at the right time and become genuine hits.

The hope for any viral campaign is that audiences will love it, share it and then buy into the product or service being advertised. Viral videos have regenerated failing brands. Old Spice, which was never much of a youth brand, has created some of the most successful viral branding campaigns of recent years and has successfully reinvigorated the brand.

5.43

5.44

5.45

5.46

5.47

5.48

5.49

5.50

5.51

5.52

5.46–5.53 **Lynx Unleash the Chaos // Soap Creative**

As this part of the Unleash the Chaos campaign for Lynx was very localized (Sydney, Australia) a video documenting the launch and audience reactions was created and released online. Because of the engaging and innovative approach of the event, the video quickly went viral online and gained a reach far beyond the original event.

5.53

143

Page takeovers

Video is widely used on the Web by marketers and advertisers who are always looking for unique ways to engage an audience and promote their products. An example of video advertising on the Web is that of the 'page takeover'. Many films, games and products have trailers, interviews and content-specific videos online, but this is an increasingly crowded marketplace. With this in mind, interactive designers created the 'page takeover'. These are adverts that integrate video into a content page on a site such as YouTube or Yahoo, but add a surprise twist and kinetic 'life' to the page. It is used in campaigns to present products in more engaging ways by breaking away from the preconceptions of how video content is viewed on a web page. The effect is usually accomplished by using Flash, which creates an invisible overlay on the page and sometimes pulls content (such as comments or images) from the live page to make it seem all the more 'real'.

Page takeovers add visual effects that can give the impression that the web page has come to life, is interacting with itself or is even falling apart. Page takeovers are online so that the sites can easily be shared and become viral if the content is fun, quirky or surprising enough. The takeovers tend to be short and rarely too intrusive to the overall page experience. Page takeovers are one approach to solving the problem of engaging a non-passive audience (web users) who are used to interacting with content rather than just watching it.

The downside to page takeovers is that although they can be an engaging marketing device, some users see them as intrusive and a disruption to their daily web experience. They also tend to be aimed more at the PC/laptop user as Flash is unavailable on some mobile devices.

5.54–5.55 **The Expendables page takeover // TVG (The Visionaire Group) with Lionsgate**

This YouTube page takeover begins with what seems to be a normal YouTube page containing an interview with Sylvester Stallone about his film *The Expendables*. As the interview progresses the video thumbnails on the right-hand side come to life as 'virtual assassins' take aim at the main video player and Stallone begins to retaliate and destroy the online environment. The sequence ends with a call to action, with Stallone asking the audience to 'share' the content.

For the project to work, the viewer has to believe this is a normal page, so when the content starts to change and interact with itself, it's a more engaging surprise.

Done properly and with imagination, this can be utilized to great effect, setting the scene for the film and creating a sense of anticipation and 'buzz'.

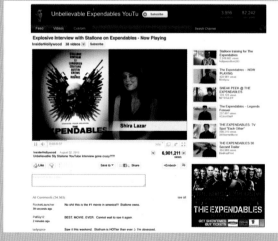

5.54

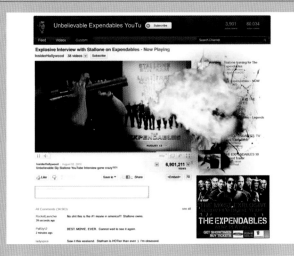

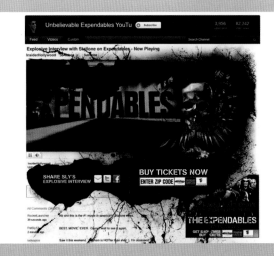

5.55

Social media

Social media is an interactive space but it's not just Facebook, it's really the world of connected devices and people. Any electronic form of two-way communication that allows for sharing of content is a social media space, from Twitter to foursquare and beyond.

The aim of social media is to connect people; brands utilize it to connect consumers to their brands. Communication technologies, such as Facebook and Twitter, are used daily by millions of people. Interactive designers have to thoroughly understand the social media space and how it can be used by clients to enable that communication.

It's not enough to put a 'like' button on a client's product and for that to ignite a traffic storm that will please the client. As with any form of communication, it's about the content. Designing with Facebook and other social media in mind is important, as we have seen from campaigns like WrestleMania from Specialmoves (which was created specifically for the social media space), but not every project can benefit from using social media. Many campaigns are entering a media space that is increasingly crowded and 'noisy'. It's innovative designers, who understand the social space, that will be able to exploit it by creating engaging projects.

Social media as a platform

Social media has undergone a revolution as brands saw the potential of connecting with millions of users. Few have been able to exploit this new space well. Zynga created *FarmVille* and other games that existed originally only on Facebook. Atto Partners in Northern Ireland made *Artwiculate*, which is a Twitter-based word game. McCann Digital in Israel used Facebook as part of an anti-drug campaign using the timeline of a drug user (called Adam Barak). These social games and campaigns have become a new platform and arena for interactive designers to work in.

Twitter is not as visually oriented as Facebook, with its more stripped down interface and the restriction of 140 characters per post, but it is about sharing and publishing user-created content. Like Facebook, it provides a platform for interaction where the users create and share content.

Facebook has become its own medium and one that (if it continues to evolve and grow) offers many challenges and opportunities for interactive designers who understand the function and appeal of social media.

5.56–5.58
Titanic 3D //
Kerve Creative

Titanic was the first advertiser page on Spotify and linked to Facebook. The project created by Kerve (UK) integrated memory, music, video and Facebook friends to create a unique multimedia experience for *Titanic* fans old and new. The project asked fans to cast their minds back to when they saw the original *Titanic* movie and then select music from that year as a soundtrack. The user's three best Facebook friends would be automatically integrated into a fan-created trailer and appear as the stars of the *Titanic* movie.

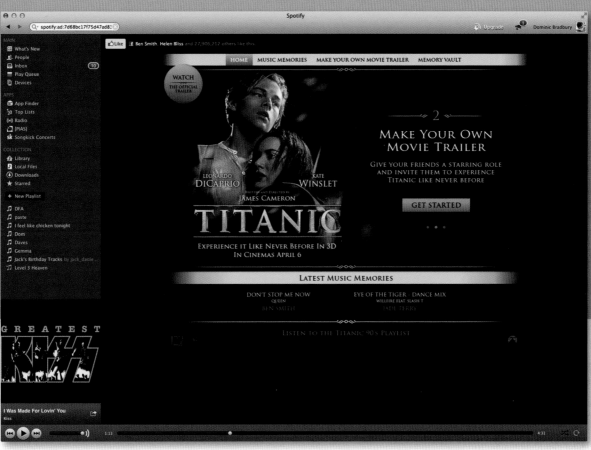

5.56

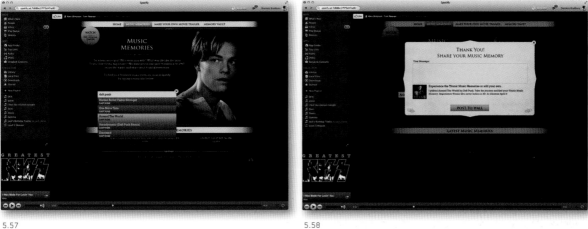

5.57

5.58

Interview: Steve Smith, senior developer

Steve Smith is a senior developer and digital director of Caramel Creative in Melbourne, Australia.

When developing an interactive project, is knowing how to code important?

It is important, but not compulsory. I personally get my kick from bringing supplied designs to life as interactive interfaces by coding in the mechanics, making things move and firing off actions and events.

With so many applications offering templates and cut 'n' paste code, why should anyone learn coding?

I find it rewarding to be able to create from scratch and know all of the ingredients that have gone into a project. It's also more secure for me in terms of knowing why a part may have broken, or if there's a bug I can fix it because I built it. It's important that designers build a system from scratch and not rely on third-party code because this is the best way to learn, and you're creating your own IP (intellectual property).

What's the best way to get started in learning how to code?

I would go to somewhere like jQuery.com and do some tutorials, or some of the iPhone development tutorials on YouTube.

I find it useful to work with other senior developers too; I can ask them questions, share the workload, as well as learn from the collaboration. Ideally, you should have an idea of what you want to make before you start, and then find out which scripting languages might be most appropriate for delivering the desired result. I would recommend learning JavaScript to begin with because it is powerful, easy to write and read, and is going to be a fundamental part of the Web moving forward into HTML5.

Which essential tips would you give to someone starting to code?

1   You'll need to be a perfect speller and an eagle-eyed reader and have a good grasp of languages in general because you could be scouring thousands of lines for one missing semi-colon or comma.
2   Aim towards learning OOP (object-oriented programming), such as JavaScript or ActionScript).

3   Be prepared to work in a constantly evolving landscape and don't worry when a new version of your language of choice makes a change. You will need to study, learn and relearn throughout your career.

4   Keep your code tidy and comment your code properly. This is important when working in a team and when returning to your code after months or years away from it.

5   Try looking one step ahead; focus on emerging technologies and think about whether you will need to be using it in the future. Prime examples are the emergence of cloud computing systems such as GitHub and frameworks for making non-native apps for iPhone and so on.

Do interactive designers who know how to code earn more?

I've always found that there have been ten designers to every coder, and interactive designers who can code are quite rare and can therefore secure better and typically higher-paid positions with less competition. Freelance interactive designers might even wish to market themselves as a coder depending on what work is available.

Some designers would say that coding is too much of a logical left-brain activity. Is coding creative?

Yes, 100 per cent! I can write some code using trigonometry that moves something around in a circle super quick and it looks great. I could paint a whole canvas of a web page with a few lines of code and make it unique every time it's loaded. Once it becomes a visual manifestation that can elicit a response, it brings graphics to life in an interesting and meaningful way.

5.59

5.60

5.59–5.60   **Surf Life Saving Squad // Ink Project, Sydney**

Even a small and seemingly simple Flash game requires coding skills to create. Any game that is engaging and fun has to go beyond simple built-in actions or pre-built code. Learning to code is important.

Case study: pq-eyewear website

Studio: Planning Unit, UK
Client: pq-eyewear

Planning Unit is a London-based creative agency. In 2011 they put together the website for pq-eyewear, featuring designs by Israeli architect and designer Ron Arad.

The designer Ron Arad had been commissioned to design a range of eyewear, and his studio came up with the concept, name, branding and brand language: pq-eyewear. It was at this point that they wanted to display the brand and its products online, so they approached Planning Unit.

The brief
The studio needed a website. The brief was: 'We have a problem, and we are coming to you to fix it'. So, it was clear from the beginning that Planning Unit had to develop the concept, purpose, design and functionality of the website.

The pitch meeting
The successful pitch was in part an outcome of a misunderstanding. The team was under the impression that it was an informal meeting to learn about the project. In fact, they were expected to show concepts and assets as if for a regular pitch, something that all the other agencies competing for the job had done. But the meeting ended up being an informal discussion. This may have appealed to Ron's sensibility and way of working collaboratively. As a result, Planning Unit were awarded the project based on this informal approach to the pitch.

'When we were shown the development work behind the eyewear designs, one of the unique aspects was Ron's sketches. They tell the story of where the designs come from.'

Jeff Knowles, Planning Unit

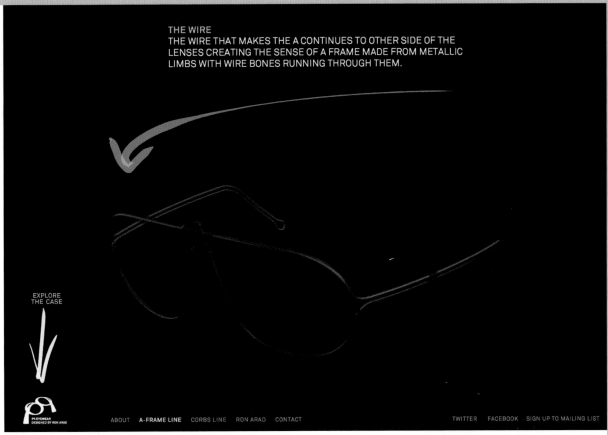

5.61

5.62

5.63

5.61–5.63 pq-eyewear website and video clips

Ron Arad is an internationally acclaimed designer; Planning Unit used videos
of Ron at work and talking about design to contextualize the web experience.

THE A
RAISE OR LOWER THE BAR THAN RUNS ACROSS THE
CENTRE OF THE A AND YOU CAN MOVE THE TWO
LENSES AND THEIR FRAMES CLOSER TOGETHER OR
FURTHER AWAY.

WHY? NO TWO HEADS ARE THE SAME SIZE AND
SHAPE, NO TWO NOSES ARE THE SAME SIZE AND
SHAPE, AND SOMETIMES NOSES GROW OVER TIME.
THE A-FRAME ALLOWS YOU TO ADJUST YOUR FRAME
TO MAKE IT FIT YOUR PARTICULAR HEAD OR
PARTICULAR NOSE PERFECTLY

EXPLORE
THE HINGE

5.64

5.64 Aesthetic and inspiration

Much of the look and aesthetic of the site was developed from Planning Unit's interaction with Ron Arad's studio. Visits to the studio gave the team a sense of the wider world of Ron Arad's design.

Initial assessment and development

The products were still in development so it was decided that the website should develop as a brand experience, giving a feel for the values of the brand that would excite people about the products. The products are not what you normally expect from eyewear, and this was reflected in Ron's designs, in not only the look but also the production methods and the functionality of the glasses.

It was felt that this was important to highlight Ron's aesthetic. The site was divided into hierarchies. Users would be greeted with large dynamic images of the glasses mixed with Ron's sketch artwork, giving the emotional connection with a high-end product. The second tier of the hierarchy would give the user an experience of the two types of glasses by using a walk through to showcase how the glasses are made and how they function. The third tier would be to drill down to view the range of glasses in detail, so users can see the different shapes and colour combinations.

Sketches as aesthetic

One of the unique aspects of the project was Ron's sketches. They tell the story of where the designs come from, and are very colourful and individual to Ron's style. These were woven into the design and aesthetic of the site. The sketches are used as full-page images, and Ron drew the navigational devices that are featured on the site, to personalize every element of the site's look and feel. This small but important detail completes the experience and conveys what the pq brand is all about.

Connecting with video

A layer of video was added to the web experience to contextualize what the brand is about, so interviews with Ron Arad were included. This simple approach communicates the deep level of thought and passion that has gone into this venture. The videos where Ron explains the ideas behind the eyewear give users an instant glimpse into the world of pq.

PROJECT TOOLS
- Adobe InDesign CS5.5
- Adobe Illustrator CS5.5
- Adobe Photoshop CS5.5

5.65

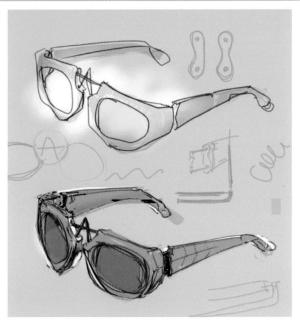

Rich media

In terms of producing the video, Ron Arad had just had a show called 'Curtain Call' running at the Roundhouse in Chalk Farm, London (UK). The Roundhouse had produced some videos about the show and Ron, and their team were happy to create the videos for the pq site. In the studio, Ron was filmed and interviewed. This material was then edited along with 3D animations of the products and some of Ron's design sketches, resulting in a cohesive bond with the website design.

Ron's creativity and vision have gone into this project, so it was important to showcase this aspect as a fundamental part of the brand. Video seemed the ideal support method as it has an immediacy that people understand.

5.65–5.66 **From sketches to prototypes**

The sketches Ron Arad used to prototype and design the eyewear became a critical aspect of the website design. They informed the navigation and the style was integrated into the feel of the site.

5.66

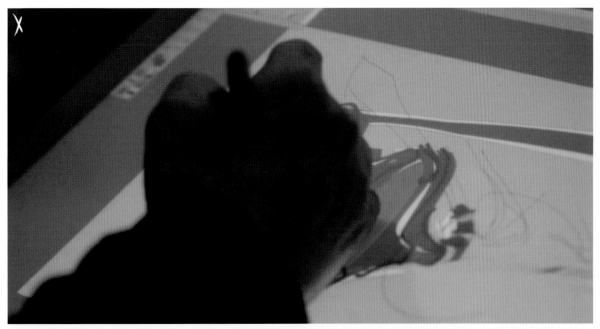

Project: Create a campaign for a TV series

The brief

Create a broadcast and online campaign for a TV series of your choice with assets that will be delivered across traditional broadcast, web-based and mobile mediums. The campaign should engage with existing fans as well as create new ones. Your choice of programme could be taken from any genre, such as horror or science fiction.

1 Create a video sting

Create a 20-second video sting for broadcast, using simple video-editing software (e.g. MovieMaker or iMovie). A sting is a short advert for a programme that establishes its personality and showcases some of its content. It's not a trailer for a specific episode, but for the whole series to get people excited about the show. As it is so short, it has to convey a lot of information and emotion.

Considerations

- Choose a programme that you know well. Recognize that the sting is not only for existing fans, but is also to encourage new fans who may not know anything about the series and characters.

- Try to fix on a theme that runs through the show and use it in the sting. The theme could be based around wacky humour, deep drama, emotions or relationships.

- Stings are short – the audience has to be grabbed very quickly and there isn't much time to build character or narrative. Clichés, stereotypes and subversions work well.

2   Create an interactive campaign concept for the TV Show

Create a mock-up for the online part of the campaign. Use assets from the show, but come up with a way of engaging audiences with innovation and experimentation. Create a presentation (using PowerPoint, Flash Catalyst, or another appropriate multimedia software) explaining the campaign and how it works.

Considerations

- What campaigns already exist? Did any of them grab you? If so, why? Can you repeat that effect?

- What interaction could be used? Would sharing clips or games help give more detailed backgrounds on the characters?

- Should the campaign run across several devices from computer-based websites to mobile apps and/or interactive billboards or screens in shopping malls?

- The campaign could integrate with a networked TV or DVR.

- Research upcoming technologies. 3D glasses, polarized glasses and touch screens are just the start. The campaign does not have to be limited by space, location or technology.

- As this is a concept it can afford to be a big idea!

Tips!

1   Video editing takes a long time, so it is important to take this into account when planning your schedule.
2   Animation takes years to get right. If you need a character consider using a friend or yourself.
3   Ensure you edit in the correct video format.
4   Remember to apply usability rules to the interactive project.

llo Cow
200 Mooney
more mooney

Bacon Cow
Cost: 200 Mooney
You need more mooney

Oil C
Cost: 200
You need mo

horn Bull
500 Mooney
more mooney

Mao Cow
Cost: 500 Mooney
You need more mooney

Bling
Cost: 10,00
This is yo

6.1

Chapter 6: Games

6.1 Cow Clicker // Ian Bogost

Cow Clicker created by Ian Bogost (US) is a Facebook game about Facebook games. It is a satirical look at how social media games make money through simple interactions. Ironically, it proved to be very popular, thus undoing the fact that it was designed to be an anti-game.

Computer games

This chapter explores how interactive designers use games to deliver engaging experiences across multimedia platforms. Interactive design studios usually create games for clients as marketing tools or promotional media, whereas a video game company traditionally creates a stand-alone product.

'Nothing's impossible.'

The Doorknob (*Alice in Wonderland*), Lewis Carroll

Many of the skills required to create video games for the entertainment industry crossover with those of interactive designers. A Flash or iPhone game could become the next big casual computer game or herald a new medium for games to enter our culture (*FarmVille* on Facebook created a new space for games). The first computer game was *Spacewar!*, developed in 1962, which ran on computers the size of large bookcases. Games are now heavily designed spaces that are used not only for entertainment, but also to educate, inform or to connect consumers with a brand.

Games can be one of the most effective methods of interactive storytelling and can directly create an emotional bond with an audience. If the game is fun, interesting, thought-provoking or innovative, an audience is likely to get hooked on the content and identify positively with the brand or message.

6.4 Jägermeister Advergames // Hi-ReS! and Playerthree

Games are a great approach to getting an audience to stay longer on a website (also known as 'stickiness'). Games engage interactively and more fully, even if it's within a branded environment. The Jägermeister *Pinball* and *Icestacker* games on the Jägermeister website encourage visitors to play around and have fun with the brand, which encourages a positive level of brand engagement.

These games were programmed by Playerthree (UK) with the games' art direction and website design by Hi-ReS! (UK).

6.2

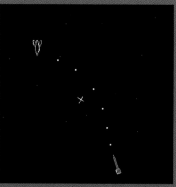

6.3

6.2–6.3 Spacewar! // Steve Russell

Games were created to run on even early computers (see image 6.2 of a PDP-1 computer). *Spacewar!* (1962) was one of the first games. It is a two-player fighter game that could be played on the PDP-1, as its operating system was the first to allow multiple users to share the computer simultaneously.

Designing games

Interactive designers may find that games are often the best routes into learning how to create engaging and emotionally resonant products. A game brings together so many different faculties and skill sets that game design is included on most interactive design courses. Over the last ten years, there has been an increase in design studios producing games for education, training or entertainment.

To know a medium is to study it. Game designers have to learn to study a game, not just play it. They must dissect and analyse the game, asking questions such as, 'Why does this game work whereas another in the same genre falls flat?', 'How does the art direction inform the story and experience?', 'What differentiates this game from its peers?'

What makes a game designer?

As with any interactive project, game design is about communication. Designers have to be able to communicate the quality of their ideas to non-technical clients or to marketing departments, as well as game testers. With something as technical as a game, designers must bring disparate groups together around the end goal of the game's experience and story. What makes a designer valuable is not the idea but being able to make that idea a reality. Game designers have to be mentally agile and lateral thinkers. They must adapt their skills as the game evolves over time, allowing new developments to inform the game **mechanic**.

The make-up of a game designer

As a rule, an experienced game designer should have knowledge of the following:

- classic literature
- myths and legends
- world religions
- art and design principles
- audio design and music principles
- variety of game genres and platforms
- solid writing skills
- life experience

The more life experience a designer has, the more that designer has to draw on to put into a game. Knowledge of how people react to stimuli and games will also inform the design process. One way to become a games designer is to make a game. Making games is the best way to learn. Every frustration, every mistake is a part of the learning process; don't wait around for the perfect idea that will set the game industry on fire, just make a game that works. Then make another one.

6.5 **The Osbournes //
Specialmoves**

One of the first big projects for Specialmoves was to create a game to promote the reality TV series *The Osbournes* in the UK. MTV Europe wanted a campaign that would be quirky and fun to reflect the tone of the TV show. Advergames were in their infancy when the team set about creating *The Osbournes*. The constraints of the technology informed the aesthetic and interaction as the team went for an 8-bit style that was part nostalgia and part innovation. *The Osbournes* won multiple awards, including a BAFTA nomination, and garnered critical acclaim and huge popularity amongst fans of the show.

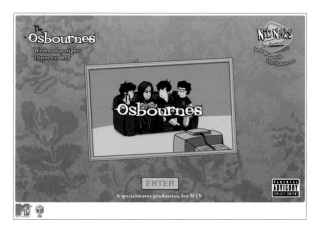
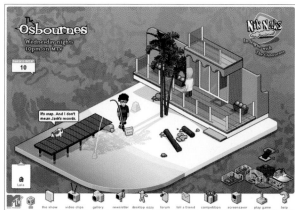

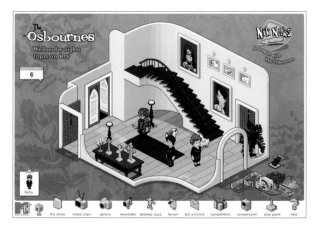

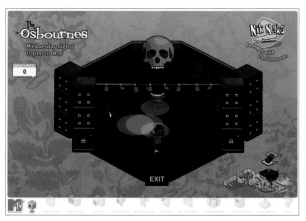

6.5

Game components

A game is a system, one that has a mechanic that defines what the game is, as well as multiple levels that allow the player to explore the world. The mechanic defines the interaction: jumping in platform games, running and gunning in first-person shooters, manipulating objects in puzzle games and so on. In his book, *The Art of Game Design*, Jesse Schell lists the four basic elements of a game: mechanics, story, aesthetics and technology.

1 *Mechanics*

Mechanics focus on how players try to achieve prescribed goals and what happens to them when they try. Mechanics are unique to the video game medium; designers must decide on which technology will best support the mechanics (e.g. first person, platform, puzzle) as well as create aesthetics consistent with the mechanics (e.g. a first-person shooter has an environment that matches that field of view).

2 *Story*

The story gives the mechanics meaning. For example, 'Why am I jumping over here?' – 'To get to the next level so that you can rescue the princess'. Narratives come in many forms, the main ones are:

(a) Pre-scripted linear narratives: these are often accompanied by video cut scenes or **FMVs (full-motion videos)**. The main narrative does not alter in reaction to the player's choices, there is only ever one ending.

(b) Non-linear or branching: these narratives are affected by player choices. The choices players make directly affect the outcome and ending they will receive on completion of the game (e.g. there were six endings to *Bioshock 2*).

(c) Emergent narrative: the narrative and world changes dependent on the player's interaction. There are effects and ramifications rippling throughout the game universe based on player decisions.

3 *Aesthetics*

Aesthetics is not just the look of the game, but is also the feel of the game. Aesthetics generate the emotional experience and connection within the game world. If a game has a certain tone or look, designers ensure that the mechanics and technology reinforce and support that aesthetic. For example, in the *Silent Hill* series (survival horror genre), fog, movement and sound effects play an important role in creating the appropriately scary atmosphere for the game.

4 *Technology*
Technology is not just about the amount of memory the console or computer has,
or how high the video resolution can go. Instead, technology is the expression
of any materials that make the game work (e.g. controllers and interfaces).
Technology that is chosen for the game will enable it to do some things and
prohibit it from doing others.

All of these elements combine in equal amounts to enable an experience for a
player. No single component is more important than the other; if one element is not
addressed properly, the game will not work or be an engaging experience.

6.6–6.7 Schell's game components

Jesse Schell (UK) breaks down video-game development into four areas: aesthetics, story, technology and
mechanics. Each area requires attention, but development necessitates trade-offs between these elements.
If the aesthetics are great but the mechanic is flawed, the game will not be successful because it will be
unplayable. If the mechanic is solid but the graphics are not great, the trade-off could still be successful. For
example, a motorbike racing game may be heavier on the physical mechanics of driving the motorbike, but
there is still a narrative aspect that gives the player a reason to win races. If the game was just riding around
aimlessly no one would want to play.

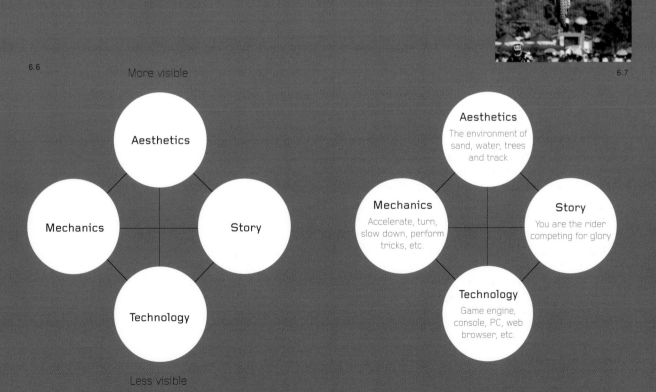

6.6

More visible

Aesthetics

Mechanics

Story

Technology

Less visible

Aesthetics
The environment of
sand, water, trees
and track

Mechanics
Accelerate, turn,
slow down, perform
tricks, etc.

Story
You are the rider
competing for glory

Technology
Game engine,
console, PC, web
browser, etc.

6.7

Games as an interactive medium

Games are often associated with large entertainment titles such as 'Call of Duty' or 'Final Fantasy'. For the interactive designer there are many other avenues into creating games for a wide spectrum of audiences.

Interactive designers are often involved with creating advergames, a term that defines the use of games to advertise or launch products. Given the enjoyable nature of games, brands know that launching a game along with a product or campaign is a great way to get the word out to a mass audience. Games used as a marketing tool add value to a brand, and associate it positively with fun, interactive and emotional experiences.

Serious games
Serious games are those that can still be fun but are more focused on training and education over selling a brand. This field contains subject matter that can involve religious games, political games, simulation and education.

Edutainment and simulation
Games can communicate a message in a way that's far more engaging to audiences than a video, lecture or other media. For example, the game *America's Army*, developed by the U.S. Army, is a free downloadable video game that looks and feels like other militaristic-style games. The difference is that America's Army is an outreach tool aimed at men and women interested in joining the U.S. Army. The production values are high, but you cannot play this game the same way you would a traditional console shooting game. The game educates the player on the goals and principles of being a U.S. Soldier.

6.8–6.14 America's Army // U.S. Army

The game *America's Army* is both a global communications initiative and an educational tool. Although the game looks like many entertainment-based PC or console shooters, this game reflects the ideologies of the U.S. Army. It's a serious game that informs, entertains and engages. The concept of *America's Army* is to create a virtual army experience, one that puts a player in realistic combat and peace-keeping roles as well as incorporating other aspects of the military. Players are bound by Rules of Engagement (ROE) with additional abilities and training 'unlocked' by engaging in teamwork and adhering to the Seven Core Army Values: loyalty, duty, respect, selfless service, honor, integrity and personal courage. Updated regularly, the virtual game reflects changes in the actual U.S. Army, both technological and directive, for example recent updates have included an emphasis on overseas contingency operations.

6.8

6.9

6.10

6.11

6.12

6.13

6.14

Casual games

Casual games are not deeply immersive worlds and do not contain large narratives, but they can be hugely popular. For example, Zynga's *FarmVille* is both a game and a new business model that netted millions in profits for the company. These forms of in-browser games have begun to interest the wider video-game industry as players are far in excess of the best-selling console games.

Casual and addictive

The growth of casual games is, in part, due to mobile devices. It's now easier than ever to use a device that is always on hand to play games. Casual games are smaller in scope than regular video games, but can still be addictive. Just because a game is seen as 'casual' does not mean they are not engaging or addictively fun. Facebook has become a medium for casual games because it draws in a social element and fits into a site that people are already using a lot. Facebook enables players to share content or high scores with their friends, which enriches the game experience. Casual games are designed to work in 'bite-sized' chunks that can be played for ten minutes or ten hours.

6.15–6.17 **Cow Clicker //
Ian Bogost**

Cow Clicker is a satirical take on casual games such as *FarmVille*. It allows a player to click on a cow every six hours (and sends out a message 'I'm clicking on a cow') for a point. Friends could invite others into their pasture and if anyone clicked on a cow, they would all earn more points. Players could spend money to get custom cows or circumvent the time restriction. It was supposed to be a pointless, frustrating game that no one would play, but would exist as a statement on the banality of some social games. However, it became a cult hit and has become a genuine social game.

6.15

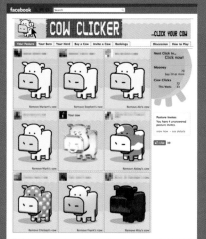

6.16

6.17

6.18

6.20

6.22

6.19

6.21

6.18–6.22 **Southern Comfort and Cola //**
Kerve Creative

The *Million Can Challenge* game was based on the fun of popping bubble wrap. Every day a consumer can open up to 300 cans in an attempt to instantly win some of the prizes offered by the Southern Comfort and Cola drink launch. As it was a Facebook app, it could be shared with friends, which enabled greater awareness for the brand. The simple mechanic of the game made it accessible and surprisingly addictive for players.

Alternate reality games (ARGs)

ARGs are a relatively new method of engaging audiences. What's misleading about the title is that 'alternate reality' actually refers to the real world. Some of the best examples of alternate reality games also happen to be marketing campaigns. The ARG has begun to be a part of the larger world of the **transmedia** experience. ARGs are split into two categories: the commercial ARG and art ARGS.

Commercial ARGs

In order to promote the video game *Halo 2*, 42 Entertainment (US) created a very different style of campaign with the ilovebees website. It was a campaign designed to coerce fans away from computer screens and to actively engage them with the world. It began with a **subliminal** web address embedded in a trailer for the *Halo* game. Observant fans who investigated the web address saw a website that appeared to have been hacked by an artificial intelligence. As the site grew and more content was loaded, the website went viral and expanded to become a form of real-life treasure hunt.

As a marketing campaign, ilovebees was the first attempt to enable an audience to find out more about a game due to be released rather than viewing a trailer or reading a review. The success of this ARG-based campaign has inspired other media, such as film, to use ARGs in advance of a release date. ARG campaigns were used for *The Dark Knight* and *Tron Legacy*.

6.23

6.23 ilovebees Halo 2 ARG // 42 Entertainment

The ARG *ilovebees* relied on fans of the upcoming *Halo 2* title to work. To get them involved it used mystery and at times quite 'old school' technology (such as phone booths) to communicate more parts of the larger mystery surrounding elements of the game.

'The concept of alternate reality is becoming more and more central to discussions about the future of games.'

Jane McGonigal, serious games designer, 'Reality is Broken' (2011)

Art ARGs

There are non-commercial art ARGs that are built as an investigation into the process and understanding of gaming itself. *Uncle Roy All Around You* was created by Blast Theory from the UK and merges the real and the virtual into a technology-enhanced game of hide-and-seek. The game lasts about an hour and involves up to 12 physical players on the streets of a real city and players online who have access to a virtual map of the city they can move in using avatars.

The players are asked to find the location of Uncle Roy's office and a disembodied Roy provides them with clues based on physical locations in the city. The street players can see the location of online players as they explore their city under direction from Uncle Roy and online players via hand-held devices. The online players can communicate with the real-world players via chat systems as the street players relay their location via GPS and audio. The online players direct the real-world players to locations of objects that help to uncover the mystery of where Uncle Roy's office is and help to uncover a mystery; the players are asked if they can make a commitment to a stranger.

Interactive designers who understand and can create games are crucial to the future of any design studio. As games continue to grow, designers have to be able to exploit the nature of this format and create new ways of playing and entertaining.

6.25

6.26

6.27

6.24

6.24–6.27 Uncle Roy All Around You // Blast Theory and Mixed Reality Lab

Uncle Roy All Around You, created by Blast Theory in collaboration with the Mixed Reality Lab, connects the physical and virtual world in a game of technological hide-and-seek via GPS, text messaging and audio feeds.

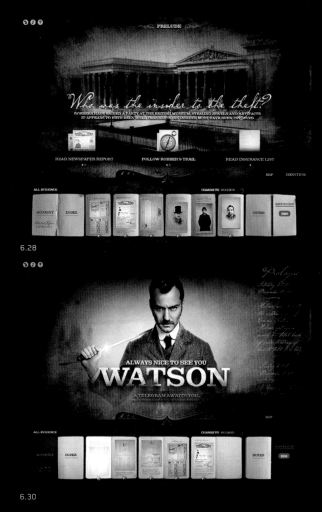

6.28

6.29

6.30

6.31

6.28–6.35 221B // AKQA

AKQA created an advergame called *221B* that mixes elements of alternative reality with a mystery game to promote the *Sherlock Holmes* movie of 2009. Players invite a Facebook friend to be their Watson and they must cooperate to solve mysteries pulled from the universe of Sherlock Holmes. Each player receives different clues, which are accessed and shared via an in-game notebook. New cases were released weekly and the game provided background on some of the characters from the movie as well as creating new narratives and cases to explore within the Holmes' universe.

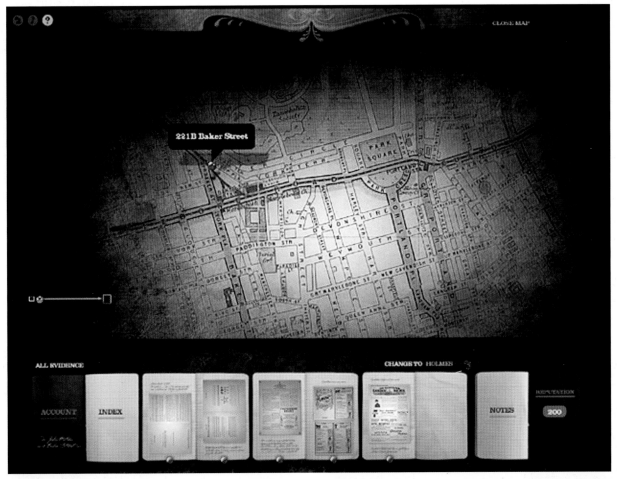

6.33

6.34

6.35

Interview: Pete Everett, advergame designer

Pete Everett is the co-founder of Playerthree in the UK, and an expert on designing advergaming projects.

What is advergaming?

In the online space, advergames drive traffic to a website. It makes sense for brands to create games and use them to promote their products. The best advergames are either subtle in their brand messaging, or so spot-on for the target market that you're not surprised to see the brand associated with the game when the branding or messaging does appear.

How do games work as a marketing strategy?

Games are a traffic driver to lure people to a website, in the hope that once there users will love what they see. Games are great for this, especially if you compare them to banner adverts. People avoid looking at banners, but they seek out games and will even share them with their friends. In terms of brand recognition, user engagement and click-through, you can get a lot more traffic to your site by creating a decent game than by launching a banner-ad campaign for the same money.

What can 'break' an advergame?

Too much branding or being too heavy handed is a bad thing, it just puts people off. This is one of the key things we do with educational games – and something we educate clients about. There's no point being too heavy handed with the educational aspect of a game. If the audience thinks it's being lectured to, people will just switch off, and you'll end up educating nobody. Better to have a big audience who love playing your game learning a little, than not learning anything at all.

How do you develop from an initial brief to a final game?

We produce a game design document that outlines basic visuals for the game mechanic, and this is signed off by the client. At this stage, we keep the description strategically vague to allow us some breathing space to add depth as the game play evolves.

The best games evolve organically during the design process. Often the details in design and nuances of interaction that are introduced later make a game memorable. Sometimes, a game that looks good on paper simply doesn't work in practice, and it's our job to quickly find a solution and still fit within the client's brief, schedule and budget.

How do you decide who is going to work on a project?

We have a team of 21 people – many of whom are multi-talented. We have a choice of visual styles from the designers, a choice of authoring environments from the coders, and a range of platforms we can export to, including web, iOS, Android and PlayStation Network (PSN). Some people have skills in certain areas (e.g. physics or AI), but we try to avoid pigeonholing people.

All our developers are game designers rather than 'coders' and this is key to the success of the games that we build. We give the developers space to add depth to the games that they create and get them on board as early as possible to influence the design.

Do you have any best practices for designing?

We have a key question: is it fun to play? If the answer is 'no', we've failed, and the game will not be delivered until it is. Occasionally, this means we miss a deadline, but I'm convinced that clients who procure our services are coming to us as game designers, and they should expect no less.

You could take all the elements of *Pac-Man* and put them together in a way that wasn't fun to play, but it takes skill to work out what is missing and add it to make it come together. That's the difference between a game developer and a coder. Some things that look good on paper just aren't fun, and that's difficult to account for on a spreadsheet. Putting the 'fun' in takes work and experience.

6.36

6.37

6.38

6.36 **Stunt Bunnies Circus // © Playerthree**
6.37 **Nom Nation // © Playerthree and Channel 4**
6.38 **Capper // © Coca-Cola**

Working on a mixture of branded advergames, educational titles and their own IP across web and handheld devices, Playerthree endeavour to make their games as accessible and easy to play as possible.

173

Case study: Coca-Cola Open the Games

Studio: Playerthree, UK
Client: Coca-Cola

The Open the Games website was a celebration of Coca-Cola's ongoing association with the Winter Olympics (2010), and the team at Playerthree worked directly with the Coca-Cola brand on this global online campaign.

Getting the client, starting the brief

Playerthree were approached by SEGA to design and build some games for the Coca-Cola brand. Coca-Cola were an official sponsor of the Winter Olympics and SEGA were a gaming partner of the Olympics.

Playerthree is a small games studio in England, so working with Coca-Cola (based in Atlanta, Georgia, USA) for such a major event was an exciting challenge. Coca-Cola needed the creative team to be very clear about what they were going to achieve before work began, so they could line up marketing and promotional material while the game was being developed.

Proving new technology

The team developed the game using the software Unity3D as a development platform. In 2010, it was still in its infancy, but as Coca-Cola wanted the games to appeal to aspirational, web-savvy, console-playing teenagers, the quality and toolset of the Unity3D engine was seen as a good fit for the demographic. It also gave the team the freedom to develop a console-quality game that worked in web browsers, utilizing an international branded game marketed alongside a global event.

Choosing the game

The client had suggested a snowboarding game (this was for the Winter Olympic Games). Members of the creative team had been playing the video game *SSX* on the PS2 and *Shaun White* on the Wii in anticipation of the contract, and the thought was that by using Unity3D, an online version of such high quality would be attainable. Knowing that the target audience for the advergame would have been playing these games too, the team knew they had to deliver as parallel an experience as possible.

6.39

6.40

6.39 Adding game depth

Depth was added to the snowboard experience via a mini-game, *Snowball Fight*. It's a four-on-four multi-player game that offered a different experience outside of the main snowboarding focus.

6.40 Custom avatars deepen engagement

Game avatars are customized by spending experience points that unlock in-game functionality, gear and snowboard designs. The game also transfers stats and artwork into social networking sites to enhance appeal.

6.41 Console level quality

6.41

Freeride is a full-on snowboarding game. Players are able to execute tricks, jumps and grabs in a 3D environment. Registered players can create custom runs that can be shared on social networks and with other players.

6.42

6.42–6.43 Character design iterations

There were multiple iterations for the game character; originally, the model was simpler and more cartoon style, but, became more detailed. The challenge was in ensuring the same level of detail in the character selection screens as in the game level.

Prototyping and wireframing

In creating a prototype, the team took a two-pronged approach – running development tests while simultaneously designing all of the wireframes, layouts and screen designs. The tests informed and shaped the designs before they were finalized and approved. When working with such a large brand, and with international teams working on other aspects of the marketing push, the project generated a huge amount of paperwork. There was a lot of project management and meetings, without which the end result would not have been possible.

Production

The name of the game was *Freeride*, so it was critical that the players would be able to start their run almost anywhere on the mountain and be able to create and share their own runs/tracks with friends. This required creating not just a snowboarding game, but also a fully functioning track designer and editor, as well as a back-end to store the tracks, players and their upgrades.

The first step was to create a snowboarder player who could slide down a mountain as a proof of concept. The team then developed the level editor and wrote all the server-side interaction. This part of the larger puzzle was crucial in ensuring that there was a smooth and solid process underpinning the game to reduce the risk of any last-minute technical hitches further down the line. Early on, the team prototype proved that the snowboarding part would be achievable so the focus was switched to the back-end.

6.43

Client coordination

The client was shown level builds and demos. The team had to be clear about exactly what they were showing to the client, what was a prototype and what was fixed in the game. The team soon learnt it was better to display bright red boxes with crosses through them for everything that wasn't finalized otherwise the client would spend too long asking about the appropriateness and fit of those graphics. Learning the levels of communication between client and creative teams was a big part of the project and a learning curve for both sides.

Technical innovation

Coca-Cola had put their faith in a small studio to create a pure gaming-led site, rather than a website with some mini-games in it. While the gameplay was emulating what a player would expect to see on a console, the game would work in a web browser.

For a browser-based game, the most innovative part of the project was the level creator and editor. The creator was designed to make it easy for players to design their own track, all players had to do was snowboard down the mountain. The application records their path, and then players can rewind back to the top of the mountain, place obstacles, trees and jumps, and then snowboard down the route again to prove it could be completed and to set the first score.

Once this route was logged, it was available for the rest of the world to play. This proved to be a very popular part of the game. It gave the player ownership over elements of the game, which became an important part of creating a positive gaming experience.

The launch

The game was received very well across the globe, both by players and media sites. The site was particularly popular in Scandinavia where the client ran special marketing promotions in line with the advergame. Coca-Cola put playable versions of the game on big screens at promotional events in Vancouver during the Winter Olympics and it became a very successful part of their overall promotion at the games. The team worked hard and really pushed the limits of what a small team can do with an online branded game.

All images copyright The Coca-Cola Company.

PROJECT TOOLS

- Basecamp: online project management
- Illustrator/Photoshop for the rest of the designs and textures
- MantisBT: an open-source bug-tracking system
- 3DS Max for the 3D modelling
- PHP for the server-side stuff
- Unity for game development

Project: Create an advergame

The brief

Design and prototype an advergame (or series of mini-games) based on re-engaging and remarketing a sports drink and brand such as Powerade (owned by Coca-Cola). Imagine Powerade wants to gain ground against its main competitor Gatorade. Come up with an engaging interactive project that will appeal to and capture a wider demographic than the traditional focus of sports players and athletes.

1 Research

Create a research document of six–eight pages. Research the brand that you have chosen and create initial sketches and ideas for the game mechanic (racing, platform, puzzle etc.) and platform (web based, ARG, mobile?). The document should include sketches, wireframes, game examples, and a survey of similar advergame campaigns.

Considerations

- Should the game be serious in tone (a 'proper sports game') or quirky stupid-fun and introduce characters that could be used across media?

- How much depth should the game have? It should be able to deliver a positive experience for the gamer immediately and over time.

- Should the game be on social media sites (casual sites like Facebook) or on a smartphone, a tablet or web-based?

2 Prototype and present

Using interactive software such as GameSalad, GameMaker, Flash Catalyst or presentation software (e.g. PowerPoint), create artwork and media that will provide a concept prototype or proof of concept of the game.

The prototype must deliver artwork, character design, level design and assets that go beyond static design to demonstrate the interactivity (mechanic, aesthetic) and scope of the game. Use multiple screen/slides/pages and overlays of art assets to imply the interaction. For example, a menu system could have working buttons in PowerPoint that when clicked jump to different slides in the presentation with different content so it would provide the look and feel of some of the interaction design.

Considerations

- Does your advergame deliver the correct message for the brand?

- What aesthetic are you going for? It could be old school 8-bit or super slick 'console' styled.

- The depth of the game is important; if it keeps people playing, it keeps people connected to the brand. Be careful not to push the brand too hard and don't overdo it.

Tips!

1 Concentrate on creating a fun advergame.
2 Make sure the game levels increase in difficulty.
3 Don't focus on a massive backstory or narrative.
4 Make it simple, but deep.

Conclusion

Achievement unlocked! Now you have a really good grasp of the fundamentals of interactive design. The past six chapters were an introduction to some of the creativity and innovation that goes into expressing design through this relatively new platform. The digital interactive space is still uncharted and as new technology develops so will the possibilities.

There is one fundamental truth in all design: an idea has to be expressed and created to be worth anything. If it stays in your head, it's meaningless – it has to be made real. To achieve this, interactive designers rely on many different skill sets and collaborators, from programmers to graphic artists and animators, so the key skill is communication and iteration. Make it, then make it better.

To be successful you must immerse yourself in the medium, making it where you live is very important. Expertise takes a long time but it's possible with small steps, books like this are a critical aid along that path. A passion for the process of design and knowledge of the wider world of design (for example, product design, industrial design and graphic design) will always inform your creative process and make you an interactive designer.

Applying research-based knowledge is a key element in problem solving; a great idea is only great if it's appropriate for the intended audience. Being able to see how other people think and use design is critical when creating interactive projects. A good designer has to bring the audience along with them, not try to force the future upon them.

Interactive design is possibly the most exciting space for designers to work in right now. As technologies become ever more portable and ubiquitous (interactivity will be everywhere from fridges to phones and wallpaper) the designer who knows this space and can exploit it for a client is going to be in much demand. The future is very bright for anyone looking for a career in this industry.

Glossary

Agency: a term that describes user interaction with an on-screen element or in the real world. Without the agency of the player, a video game character does nothing.

Animatic: an animated storyboard. This is the next stage on from a static storyboard. An animatic allows the team to see how the motion and timing of the piece will work.

Animatronics: mechanical machine that simulates natural movement and subjects (e.g. dinosaurs or presidents in theme park attractions).

Application development: the development of a software product; includes programming, research, prototyping and software testing.

Application programming interface (API): a software component or tool that allows software to 'talk' to each other. So a Google 'API' allows a programmer to connect their website to Google's data and to pull that content from Google onto their page.

Back-end developers: programmers who create the technical engine that runs the project and may write the code. For example, on a website, the back-end team would be working with languages such as PHP/Python/ Ruby that may be used for a shopping cart or a search engine.

Brainstorming: a tool for opening up a free-association discussion for ideas.

Brief: a document that outlines a design project, usually assigned by the client. It focuses on outcomes, not the aesthetic or technology involved in creating the project.

Click-through: a measurement of the level of engagement with an online advert. A successful ad will have a high click-through rate as it drives audiences towards the advertised content.

CMYK *(see RGB)*

Compilers: a computer program that transforms code written in one programming language (C++, C#) into another computer language that a computer can use. Most commonly used to create an executable programme that runs on an operating system (OS).

Compositing: combining elements into one image or video, for example, the 'green screen' an actor is shot against is replaced later with an animated/film scene. Or the combining of visual effects, an explosion or supernatural effect into a scene.

Comps: a rough design layout (often in print) presented to the client by the design team. It will be a sketch of the design layout and often contains 'placeholder' content (not the finalized designs).

Contextual enquiry: real-life testing of a project; the data gathered from a real person interacting with a prototype and giving feedback to the team.

Creative Commons: a copyright and licence structure that favours sharing of services and products for the explicit use of remixing, sharing and distributing. There are some commercial restrictions.

Crowd-sourced: using (usually online) communities to solve problems or create content. Wikipedia is an example of a crowd-sourced knowledge repository. Anyone can post and correct/edit articles, and add to the knowledge base.

CSS (cascading style sheets): advanced layout language for a website. It describes how the site is viewed, from defining margins and text colour, to the font and overall layout.

Dubbing: in post-production of a video or animation it's the process of recording and replacing an actor's voice with the one shot on location. Dubbing is used because a location or studio shoot cannot always capture 'clean' versions of the voice or sound.

FMV (full motion video): in the context of a video game it refers to moments in a game that the player cannot control and are often used as exposition to drive the narrative forward.

Focus groups: used in marketing as a method of analysing and capturing data from people on their reaction to a product or project.

Front-end designers: programmers or design/code crossover people who work with a variety of languages from ActionScript (for Flash) to web languages such as HTML/ CSS or JavaScript. They work with scripting that affects the look, aesthetic and interaction of the project. This could be the CSS scripts that create the layout of a website or the ActionScript that makes an advergame work.

HTML (HyperText Markup Language): the programming language of the World Wide Web; an HTML page is delivered by the web server to a web browser, which translates the HTML into the web page.

Ident: station/broadcast identification image. For example, BBC or CBS logo, at the bottom of the TV image. Also known as 'stingers' – the videos that play before a programme.

Interface design: in this context, it is the design of a system (menus, navigation, control mechanisms) that communicates between the user and the application/software. It can also apply to hardware (the play button on a DVD player is an interface). Also known as GUI or graphical user interface.

Lexicon: visual or verbal vocabulary of a language or culture.

Mechanic: in the context of a game, it is the physics or heart of how the game is played. The 'jumping' mechanic defines a platform video game such as *Super Mario*.

Metrics: the measurement of the performance of a project, often used in video games to measure and define where players are spending time, getting stuck, using certain skills or weapons etc. Metrics also can measure the success of the advertisement in advergaming, and it's also used in project management to assess the value of a project against the criteria of time, cost, resources, scope, quality and actions.

Motion graphics: moving animation, audio and/or video that combine to create an engaging visual communication project. Motion graphics usually imply 2D or 3D 'graphics' such as text, diagrams, logos and idents over narrative or Disney-style animations or films.

Open source: Software and hardware that are community created and offered for free to the world by its creators, for others to share or update on a variety of Creative Commons licences (e.g. the Linux operating system).

Persona: a fictional profile created by a team (sometimes marketing) that details a potential user of the product. The best way of thinking of a persona is by creating a Facebook profile and content for the intended audience who will use the project.

Physical computing: the use of electronic components and code/programming to create an interactive environment to engage audiences outside of a computer monitor (e. g. Processing, Arduino and PureData).

Pixel density and screen sizes: people usually sit 70 cm (27.5 inches) from a computer screen so the pixel density (PPI) can be 110 PPI and images still look good. Computer monitors didn't increase pixel density much, they just got physically larger. Early smartphones and tablets had to get around the issue of small/tiny screens and users wanting readable text and sharp images. So they upped the pixel density – more image information in a smaller space. Newer mobile devices continue to increase the pixel density as the physical size of such devices cannot change much.

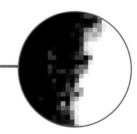

7.1

7.1 Pixel density

Most people usually sit 70cm (27.5 inches) from a computer screen, the pixel density (PPI) can be 110PPI and images will still look good at that distance. However, early smartphones and tablets had to get around the issue of small screens and users wanting readable text and sharp images at very close proximity. So they upped the pixel density – more information in a smaller space.

7.2 7.3

RGB – additive **CMYK – subtractive**

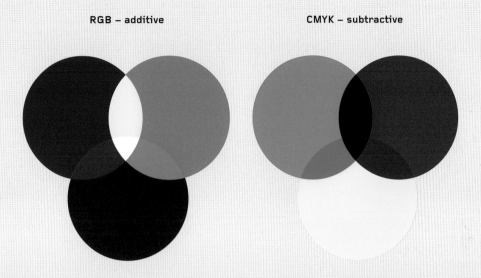

7.2–7.3 **RGB and CMYK colour schemes**

RGB is an additive system (monitors emit light) going from black to white. CMYK is a subtractive system and begins with white, mixing colours until black.

Post-production: in video, animation and film, this is the process of creating the final look and aesthetic of the production. It includes compositing real-life shots with special effects, colour-fixing the footage, and adding titles.

Project owner: the voice of the client and the studio. The role ensures the project is delivering on the goals and values of the client. The project owner also creates customer-centric content such as user stories, storyboards and presentations.

Proof of concept: a very rough technical prototype that shows the bare bones of how a project will technically work. It's enough interaction to prove the viability of the project.

Responsive design: usually refers to websites, it's the design and creation of a site/product that adapts to the environment it is being used in. So a website would be content optimized for delivery across mobile, computer monitor and tablet platforms.

RGB: There are two colour schemes used in digital design, RGB (red, green and blue) and CMYK (cyan, magenta, yellow and black). The main difference between them is that RGB is used for anything that is shown on a screen (for example, web pages, videos and games) and CMYK is used in print.

Computer monitors use RGB natively, it's how they display colour to the eye; it's an 'additive' system, which is where colours are created by mixing light emitted from differently coloured sources. As an additive system, RGB colours begin at black and white is added to create the range of colours across the spectrum (see images 7.2–7.3).

CMYK is a subtractive system. Traditionally. it comes from the mixing of paints, dyes and inks to create a full range of colours. Each colour is created by effectively subtracting wavelengths of light and reflecting the remainder. CMYK starts at true white and then 'subtracts' colours to create a full range of colours.

A computer monitor emits light from its LEDs, whereas ink on paper absorbs or filters specific colour wavelengths. The result is that images displayed on a computer monitor may differ quite radically from what is seen on paper via a printer. When working for print, the design application must be using the CMYK colour space (these are available in Photoshop, Illustrator and InDesign for example) and ideally, the monitor should be colour calibrated to the printer for the best results.

183

Resolution: An image has a certain number of pixels across and a certain number of pixels in depth. Depending on how many pixels per inch this is displayed or printed at dictates the image size. Halving the PPI of an image doesn't however halve the image size, as can be seen below. Taking an image from 300 PPI (normal print resolution) to 150 PPI quarters the image size (see images 7.4–7.5).

Scenario: expanding on the use of the persona, the scenario imagines how this person will use the product and posits potential usability shortfalls or design flaws.

Semantics: the study of the meaning of language as expressed through words. It can also be used in relation to programming, for example, the programming language C++ has its own defined semantics that a programmer has to learn to be able to work with the code.

Semiotics: the study of the meaning associated with signs and symbols. It looks at how a message is communicated through a symbol based on its context in a situation, and also how that can be transferred into a different context whilst retaining meaning.

Smart devices: an 'always on' device that is connected to a network. It is transportable (e.g. mobiles, tablets and laptops) and also capable of voice, video and data communication.

Subliminal: a subconscious perception of an image, sound or video, often because it is shown very quickly, but is still perceived by the audience.

Team: designers and developers responsible for delivery of the project: research, analysis, testing and production.

Transmedia: associated with expanded storytelling, it's defined as one story that is delivered across multiple media and outlets. The story can come from a TV show, film, video game or product. A transmedia project will expand on areas of the narrative not explored in the main medium.

7.4–7.6 Size versus resolution

The size of a digital image is measured in pixels. The height and width correlate to the physical size of an image in centimetres or inches when printed out. Resolution, or pixels per inch (PPI), denotes the quality of an image when it's printed. The higher the PPI the more information and, therefore, the better the quality of the image.

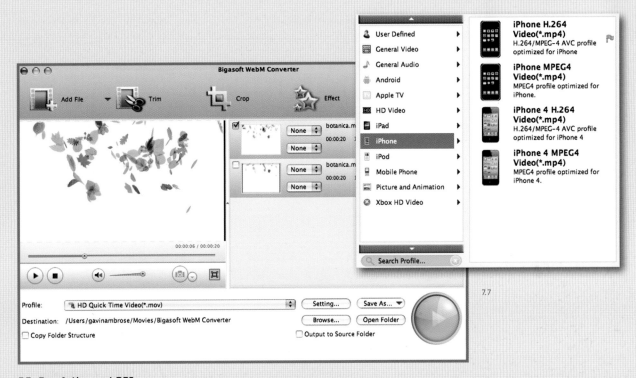

7.7

7.7 Resolution and PPI

It is important to understand resolution and how displays work. There is no standard screen size or pixel-depth for a smartphone, tablet or computer monitor. Learning about different resolutions and PPI will be critical when delivering projects for multiple devices.

Ubiquitous computing: the move towards computers embedded in everything and used by everyone. These devices will be able to communicate with us, and with each other (e.g. smartphones).

Usability: the practice of designing an interface or product with the end user in mind. Although the interface may make total sense to the designer, it may not work for everyone. So when it's 'user tested', flaws in the design can be addressed through usability testing.

Usability designer: designers (often interactive) who concentrate on how the product will be used and design the product in accordance with how the user will use it.

User experience design (UX): concentrates on the experience based on cultural relevance, ease of use, efficiency and worth of the design to the user.

User-generated content (USG): the dynamic Web where content is created by the audience and shared with others. For example, the content may be on a blog, Facebook, Flickr or YouTube.

User stories: an approach to imagine how users would engage with the project, based on their predefined attitudes and personality traits.

Virals: edgy, often controversial, short advertisements that are usually only experienced online. They are created to have maximum impact and are designed to 'go viral' as the goal is to make the audience share the link/video with everyone on their social network, spreading the campaign's message.

Wayfinding: the study of how people or crowds orient themselves and get to and from a destination.

Wireframes: a form of rough layout that shows the interactive content and flow of the navigation in a product, such as mobile phone apps or websites. For example, what button leads to which content and how does the user get back to the start?

Zeitgeist: the general cultural climate within a nation or cultural group. It can be thought of as 'whatever is hot right now' in the media, entertainment, advertising, art and design.

7.8   7.9   7.10   7.11

Red channel   Green channel   Blue channel   RGB image

7.8–7.11 RGB channels

An image is made up of one, two, three or four channels, depending on whether it is a greyscale, a duotone, an RGB image or a CMYK image.

Technical glossary

Alpha channel: a portion of every pixel's data is reserved for transparency. RGB images (e.g. in Photoshop) contain four channels: red, green and blue (RGB) and one alpha channel. The alpha channel identifies how the pixel colours in the image should be merged when they are overlaid. It is also referred to as the 'transparency channel'.

AVI (Audio Video Interleave): a video format created by Microsoft and native to the Windows environment.

FLA: native Adobe Flash file, these are often much larger than the compressed, exported SWF files used on websites.

GIF (Graphics Interchange Format): rarely used as it's a low resolution bitmap format. It was created for very low bandwidth web pages in the earliest days of the Web. It remains popular because it can be used as a rudimentary animation format. Simple frames can be created then displayed on a web page as an animation.

Image formats and extension

An 'extension' is the three letters after a file name that denote the application it was created in, or the format of the file. So 'myfile.doc' would be a document created in Microsoft Word, whereas 'myfile.jpg' is an image file in JPG format.

JPG (Joint Photographic Experts Group): a lossy compression format for bitmaps such as photographs. JPG compresses an image to make it easier to transport or share.

Lossy: means that information, in this case pixels, are stripped out of the original file to make it smaller.

MOV: an Apple QuickTime movie file that can be played using a QuickTime player and is native to the Mac.

PDF (Portable Data Format): a document that embeds the text, fonts, graphics and other information so that anyone can read it.

PNG (Portable Network Graphics): created to circumvent licensing issues that arose from the GIF format. PNG has a transparency layer option and can be low or high quality.

.PSD (Photoshop Data file): the format used by Adobe Photoshop and can only be edited in that application.

RAW: available on some DSLR cameras, the RAW format is lossless or nearly-lossless compression. It produces high-quality files that are much smaller than TIFFs.

SVG (Scalable Vector Graphics): an open standard all-purpose vector format designed for the Web and other media platforms.

SWF (pronounced 'swiff'): the web-ready default output of a Flash file, it incorporates images, animation scripts, sounds and fonts for embedding into a web page.

TIFF (Tagged Image File Format): a file that can be uncompressed and used for large high-quality images. Most high-end scanners and some DSLR cameras capture in TIFF format. TIFF also supports CMYK so is used for print-ready graphics and images.

Videos

Video can be output in several ways and much like images they have their own compression algorithms known as codecs. There are two types of codec, lossless and lossy and two methods of using them, authoring (usually lossless) and delivery (usually lossy).

A lossless video file is the raw recorded footage, the codec is the format of the file, for example it would commonly be an .AVI file on a Windows PC or a .MOV QuickTime file on a Macintosh. Very few cameras record to these formats so an intermediary codec is used, usually MPEG or a variant of it.

A lossy codec will compress a file size down to fit on a variety of media, most commonly using the MPEG format, similar to the recognizable MPEG-3 (or MP3) music file.

Some High Definition (HD) cameras record to a specific HD format AVCHD; the manufacturers Canon, Panasonic and Sony have cameras that use AVCHD. This is another form of codec; the camera is using internal hardware to compress the video footage on the storage medium of the camera. It's then uncompressed when it's imported to an editing application.

Authoring codecs

Authoring codecs preserve image quality for editing purposes, the higher and better quality the original, the more systems the video can be delivered on. A high-definition video can go straight out to Blu-ray or be compressed for low-bandwidth users on YouTube.

Because of their very large files size and lack of general hardware support, authoring codecs are used in editing suites and then exported out to the common delivery formats.

Animation: lossless codec developed by Apple for QuickTime and supports an alpha channel. Works well with traditional 2D animations.

DV: DV-NTSC, the 720 x 480-pixel default DV codec that comes installed with QuickTime for use in accordance with the North American broadcast standard and DV-PAL, the 720 x 576 also available for European playback standards. DV can be AVI or MOV standards.

DVCPRO, DVCAM, DVCPRO 50 and DVCPRO HD: types of high-quality DV format that were developed by camera manufacturers Sony and Panasonic. Most editing applications support these DV types.

Delivery codecs

When exporting to a specific format for a device (DVD player or online) these codecs provide the balance between small file sizes and the best image quality. The main three codecs are:

FLV/VP6: Flash video is used in many online spaces because of its ability to compress video intensely while maintaining video quality. Used by YouTube and Vimeo.

H.264 (MP4/M4V): really great file size to quality ratio. The files are bigger than FLV or MPG2 but still look very good especially when compressing massive HD files. Used extensively on the Mac platform.

WMV 9: is a very flexible codec that allows video to scale from mobile devices to high-definition DVD. More Windows PC friendly than Mac.

These three codecs are often exported in different 'wrappers' for delivery on a multitude of devices and systems, so an H.264 file may be an MP4 file for a play on a PlayStation 3 or M4V for play in iTunes. Increasingly almost any video format can be played on any device.

DivX, Xvid, FFmpeg and 3ivx: these are different implementations of the MPEG-4 (MP4) codec. Commonly used to compress and distribute video files online for download. Many DVD players have the DivX version of the MPEG-4 codec built into them.

MPEG-2 (MP2): used on DVD, SVCD and standard definition digital or cable broadcasting.

MPEG-4 (MP4): latest and highest definition compression it's used for online video, broadcast and storage media. MPEG-4 offers improved quality from MPEG-2 and is an HD format. Also seen in the H.264/AVC HD codecs.

VC-1: (WMV 9) video codec: one of the three video codecs in Blu-ray high-definition optical disc standards based on Microsoft WMV 9 compression.

NTSC and PAL

NTSC and PAL are two broadcast formats used internationally. NTSC (National Television Standards Committee) is used in North America and most of South America as well as Japan. PAL (Phase Alternating Line) is used in Europe, Australia and parts of Asia.

The main differences are in the amount of Frames per Second (FPS) and scan lines sent out (for old non-digital TVs). With NTSC 30 frames are transmitted each second with 525 scan lines. PAL has 25 frames per second with 625 scan lines.

You cannot play an NTSC format video on a PAL television and vice versa. There are workarounds but, like electricity being different in various parts of the world, a converter is required.

Digital solves many of the problems of NTSC vs PAL in the non-broadcast world, an MPEG will play on most computers.

Bibliography

Ambrose, G. and Harris, P. (2008), *The Fundamentals of Graphic Design*. AVA Publishing.

Barnum, C.M. (2010) *Usability Testing Essentials: Ready, Set...Test!*. Morgan Kaufmann.

Bergeron, B. (2006) *Developing Serious Games (Charles River Media Game Development)*. Charles River Media.

Bergström, B. (2009) *Essentials of Visual Communication*. Laurence King Publishing.

Bogost, I. (2011) *How to Do Things with Videogames*. University of Minnesota Press.

Bogost, I. (2010) *Persuasive Games: The Expressive Power of Videogames*. The MIT Press.

Buxton, B. (2007) *Sketching User Experiences: Getting the Design Right and the Right Design (Interactive Technologies)*. Morgan Kaufmann.

Chandler, C., Unger, R. (2009) *A Project Guide to UX Design: For user experience designers in the field or in the making*. New Riders Press.

Cohen, M., Jacobs, S., Plaisant, C. and Shneiderman, B. (2009) *Designing the User Interface: Strategies for Effective Human-Computer Interaction*. Addison Wesley.

Coughter, P. (2012) *The Art of the Pitch: Persuasion and Presentation Skills that Win Business*. Palgrave Macmillan.

Heath, C. and Heath, D. (2007) *Made to Stick: Why Some Ideas Survive and Others Die*. Random House.

Heller, S., Vienne, V. (2009) *Art Direction Explained, At Last!* Laurence King Publishing.

Ingledew, J. (2011) *An A–Z of Visual Ideas: How to Solve Any Creative Brief*. Laurence King Publishing.

Jesper J. (2012) *A Casual Revolution: Reinventing Video Games and Their Players*. The MIT Press.

Koster, R. (2004) *A Theory of Fun for Game Design*. Paraglyph Press.

Krug, S. (2005) *Don't Make Me Think: A Common Sense Approach to Web Usability*. New Riders Press.

Krug, S. (2009) *Rocket Surgery Made Easy: The Do-It-Yourself Guide to Finding and Fixing Usability Problems*. New Riders Press.

Lessig, L. (2009) *Remix Culture*. Penguin.

Matthew, R. A. (2011) *Mining the Social Web: Analyzing Data from Facebook, Twitter, LinkedIn, and Other Social Media Sites*. O'Reilly Media.

McGonigal, J. (2011) *Reality Is Broken: Why Games Make Us Better and How They Can Change the World*. Penguin Press HC.

Montola, M., Stenros. J., Waern, A. (2009) *Pervasive Games: Theory and Design*. Morgan Kaufmann.

Mulder, S., Yaar, Z. (2006) *The User Is Always Right: A Practical Guide to Creating and Using Personas for the Web*. New Riders Press.

Munari, B. (2009) *Design As Art*. Penguin Global.

Nalty, K. H. (2010) *Beyond Viral: How to Attract Customers, Promote Your Brand, and Make Money with Online Video*. John Wiley & Sons.

Norman, D. A. (2002) *The Design of Everyday Things*. Basic Books.

Pratten, B. (2011) *Getting Started in Transmedia Storytelling: A Practical Guide for Beginners*. CreateSpace.

Qualman, E. (2010) *Socialnomics: How Social Media Transforms the Way We Live and Do Business*. John Wiley & Sons.

Rose, F. (2011) *The Art of Immersion: How the Digital Generation Is Remaking Hollywood, Madison Avenue, and the Way We Tell Stories*. W.W. Norton & Company.

Rouse III, R. (2004) *Game Design: Theory and Practice*. Jones & Bartlett Publishers.

Salen, K., Zimmerman, E. (2003) *Rules of Play: Game Design Fundamentals*. The MIT Press.

Schell, J. (2008) *The Art of Game Design: A book of lenses*. Morgan Kaufmann.

Taylor, A. (2010) *Design Essentials for the Motion Media Artist: A Practical Guide to Principles & Techniques*. Focal Press.

Trefry, G. (2010) *Casual Game Design: Designing Play for the Gamer in All of Us*. Morgan Kaufmann.

Web sources
Advergaming

Jaffe, J. (2003) *Advergaming Equals Attention* www.imediaconnection.com

Obringer, L. (2007) *How Advergaming Works* www.money.howstuffworks.com

Rodgers, A. L. (2002) *More Than a Game* www.fastcompany.com

Design documentation

Olshavsky, R. (2003) *Six Tips for Improving Your Design Documentation* www.boxesandarrows.com

Design inspiration

Belsky, S. (2010) *Five Tips For Making Ideas Happen* www.smashingmagazine.com

Boag, P. (2010) *(Web) Designers, Don't Do It Alone* www.smashingmagazine.com

Chapman, C. (2009) *100 Great Resources for Design Inspiration*
www.mashable.com

Gothelf, J, (2011) *Demystifying Design*
www.alistapart.com

Jacobs, D. (2011) *Reigniting your creative spark*
www.alistapart.com

Game design

Allmer, M. (2009) T*he 13 Basic Principles of Gameplay Design*
www.gamasutra.com

Andersen, M. (2011) *Cautionary Tales in Transmedia Storytelling*
www.wired.com

Andersen, M. (2010) *The Year in Alternate Reality Games*
www.wired.com

Bogost, I. (2009) *Persuasive Games: This Is Only A Drill*
www.gamasutra.com

Duffy, J. (2009) *Game Design, An Introduction*
www.gamecareerguide.com

Hsia, L. (2011) *How Transmedia Storytelling Is Changing TV*
www.mashable.com

Luban, P. (2011) *The Design of Free-To-Play Games: Part 1 & 2*
www.gamasutra.com

Terdiman, D. (2004) *I Love Bees Game a Surprise Hit*
www.wired.com

Thomsen, M. (2010) *Games With The Power To Offend: Surviving And Stoking Controversy*
www.gamasutra.com

Motion graphics/video

Campbell, N., Wignall, J. (2009) *How to Get into Motion Graphics Design* (video)
www.motionographer.com

Jenett, D. (2002) *Motion Design, the Future*
www.digital-web.com

Personas

Hinton, A. (2008) *Personas and the Role of Design Documentation*
www.boxesandarrows.com

Olsen, G. (2004) *Making Personas More Powerful: Details to Drive Strategic and Tactical Design*
www.boxesandarrows.com

Olsen, G. (2004) *Persona Creation and Usage Toolkit* (pdf)
www.interactionbydesign.com

Walter, A. (2011) *Personality in Design*
www.alistapart.com

Pitches

Hodges, D., Seller, J. (2010) *From pitch to launch* (video) www.aiga.org

Matson Knapp, P. (2008) *Making the Perfect Pitch*
www.howdesign.com

Smaby, K. (2011) *Being Human is Good Business*
www.alistapart.com

Protyping

Kelly, M. (2007) *Interactive Prototypes with PowerPoint*
www.boxesandarrows.com

Mall, D. (2010) *Art Direction and Design*
www.alistapart.com

Sketching

Rohde, M. (2011) *Sketching: the Visual Thinking Power Tool*
www.alistapart.com

Usability

Gaines, K. (2011) *Designing for your target audience*
www.webdesignerdepot.com

MacGowan, B. (2010) *Usability Do's And Don'ts For Interactive Design*
www.smashingmagazine.com

Nuschke, P. (2008) *Quick Turnaround Usability Testing*
www.boxesandarrows.com

Perfetti, C. (2010) *Media Usability Design*
www.perfettimedia.com

Thornton, C. (2012) *Got Usability? Talking with Jakob Nielsen*
www.boxesandarrows.com

UX design

Bolt, N. Tulathimutte, T. (2009) *Researching Video Games the UX Way*
www.boxesandarrows.com

Lazaris, L. (2010) *A Design Is Only As Deep As It Is Usable*
http://uxdesign.smashingmagazine.com

Travis, D. (2012) *Persuasion Triggers in Web Design* http://uxdesign.smashingmagazine.com

Viral video

Lehrer, J. (2011) *Why Do Viral Video Go Viral?*
www.wired.com

Useful resources

AIGA: the professional association for design
www.aiga.org

Boxes and Arrows: the practice, innovation, and discussion of design
www.boxesandarrows.com

Brand Republic: connecting advertising, marketing and PR
www.brandrepublic.com

British Design and Art Direction
www.dandad.org

Code questions
www.stackoverflow.com

Creativity online: repository of design
www.creativity-online.com

For people who make websites
www.alistapart.com

Interactivity and web-based design
www.smashingmagazine.com

Video tutorials from Adobe
http://tv.adobe.com

Video tutorials on a variety of software techniques and applications
www.creativecow.net

Index

Picture credits

Pages 8, 32–7: Specialmoves and Wieden+Kennedy: www.specialmoves.com // www.wk.com
Pages 11–3, 18–9: Big Spaceship. www.bigspaceship.com
Pages 14–15, 30, 51, 170–1: AKQA. www.akqa.com
Pages 16–7, 49, 141–3 and cover image: Soap Creative. www.soapcreative.com
Pages 21, 25, 83–7, 90, 95, 103, 161: Specialmoves. www.specialmoves.com
Pages 22–3: KesselsKramer (Hans Brinker Budget Hotel). www.kesselskramer.com
Page 27: Caius Eugene. www.caiuseugene.co.uk
Pages 29, 40, 52–3, 112, 118–9: Kokokaka. www.kokokaka.com
Page 31: Mint Digital. www.mintdigital.com
Pages 42–5: Courtesy of IDEO. www.ideo.com
Page 48: Mike Rohde/RohDesign/ Northwoods Software Development. www.rohdesign.com // www.northwoodsoft.com
Page 55: Second Story and Donna Lawrence Productions. www.secondstory.com // www.dlproductions.com
Pages 56–7: SOLID Interactive © Population Action International. www.thinksolid.com
Pages 58–9, 122–3: Second Story. www.secondstory.com
Pages 60–1: Studio La Flama/Luis Torres/ JWT. www.laflama.tv // www.jwt.com
Page 63: Emil Picasso Gentolizo. www.mobileandtabletsolutions.com
Pages 65–7: SOLID Interactive © Fresh Inc. www.thinksolid.com
Pages 70–5, 80–1, 130–1: Studio La Flama. www.laflama.tv
Page 77: designsuperbuild. www.designsuperbuild.com
Page 97: © Dieter Rams (provided by Vitsoe). www.vitsoe.com/gb/about/good-design
Page 100: Hans-Werner Hunziker (Wiki Commons).
Pages 105–9: Future Platforms. www.futureplatforms.com
Pages 115, 120–1: The One Off. www.theoneoff.com
Pages 116–7: Second Story and Snibbe Interactive: www.secondstory.com // www.snibbeinteractive.com
Pages 124–5: Julian Oliver. www.julianoliver.com

Pages 127–9: Appshaker. www.appshaker.co.uk
Pages 132–7: Krystal Schultheiss. www.krystalschultheiss.com
Page 139: Studio Output. www.studio-output.com
Pages 144–5: TVG (The Visionaire Group) with Lionsgate. www.tvgla.com
Page 147, 167: Kerve Creative Ltd. www.kerve.co.uk
Page 149: Ink Project (Sydney), for Surf Life Savers Australia. www.inkproject.com
Pages 151–3: Planning Unit for pq-eyewear and Ron Arad. www.planningunit.co.uk
Pages 156, 166: Ian Bogost. www.bogost.com
Page 158: Steve Russell.
Page 159: Playerthree and Hi ReS!. www.playerthree.com // www.hi-res.net
Page 163: taelove7 / Shutterstock.com
Page 165: America's Army/U.S. Army. www.americasarmy.com
Page 168: Andrew Sorcini, aka mrbabyman.
Page 169: Blast Theory in collaboration with the Mixed Reality Lab. www.blasttheory.co.uk // www.mixedrealitylab.org
Pages 173–7: Playerthree for Coca-Cola © The Coca-Cola Company: (*Capper* and *Open the Games* images) www.playerthree.com
Page 173: Playerthree with Channel 4: (Nom Nation image). www.playerthree.com

Acknowledgements

The authors and publisher would like to thank the following studios and designers for their help and support with this project:

Ron Arad, Julian Oliver, David Burrows at designsuperbuild; Utku Can and Angie Maguire at Mint Digital; Caroline Taylor and the team at Specialmoves; Bradley Eldridge at Soap Creative; Pete Everett at Playerthree; Jeff Knowles at Planning Unit; Jesse McCabe at SOLID Interactive, Lydia Swangren and Emil Picasso Gentolizo; Darrell Wilkins; Trevor May at Ribot; Krystal Schultheiss, Steve Smith at Caramel Creative; Stefanie Krukowski, Ashley Stewart and Zoe Conover at Powell Communications, Lori Mezoff at America's Army, Lizzie Dewhurst at AKQA, Ian Bogost, Julie Beeler at Second Story, the creative team at Future Platforms, Alex Poulson and Adam Trost at Appshaker, Dan Lamont at Blast Theory and the Mixed Reality Lab; Angie Maquire and the creative team at Mint Digital; Mike Rohde at Rohdesign; Luis Torres at Studio LaFlama; Michael Lebowitz and the team at Big Spaceship; Hugo Bergström, Daniel Strandman, Sooki Song and the creative team at Kokokaka. All the super creative people at KesselsKramer including Diana Dekker, Jurian Strik and Angela Verduin. Hayley Eynon and the team at The One Off. ; Denise Jacobs, A List Apart. com; Katrin Klausecker Nadine Stares at IDEO; Jesse Schell.

Also a big thank you to Jack Merrell, Caius Eugene and Pascal Auberson. Joe Nash for some early pointers and Will Bakali for some UX help. Jacqueline Salmond for all her help.

The publishers would like to thank Rhiannon Robinson, Dave Wood, Colin Davies and Jess Larson.

Lynne Elvins/Naomi Goulder

Working with ethics

The Fundamentals
of Interactive
Design

Ethical: aware-
ness/
reflect-
ion/
debate

Ethics is a complex subject that interlaces the idea of responsibilities to society with a wide range of considerations relevant to the character and happiness of the individual. It concerns virtues of compassion, loyalty and strength, but also of confidence, imagination, humour and optimism. As introduced in ancient Greek philosophy, the fundamental ethical question is: *what should I do?* How we might pursue a 'good' life not only raises moral concerns about the effects of our actions on others, but also personal concerns about our own integrity.

In modern times the most important and controversial questions in ethics have been the moral ones. With growing populations and improvements in mobility and communications, it is not surprising that considerations about how to structure our lives together on the planet should come to the forefront. For visual artists and communicators, it should be no surprise that these considerations will enter into the creative process.

Some ethical considerations are already enshrined in government laws and regulations or in professional codes of conduct. For example, plagiarism and breaches of confidentiality can be punishable offences. Legislation in various nations makes it unlawful to exclude people with disabilities from accessing information or spaces. The trade of ivory as a material has been banned in many countries. In these cases, a clear line has been drawn under what is unacceptable.

But most ethical matters remain open to debate, among experts and lay-people alike, and in the end we have to make our own choices on the basis of our own guiding principles or values. Is it more ethical to work for a charity than for a commercial company? Is it unethical to create something that others find ugly or offensive?

Specific questions such as these may lead to other questions that are more abstract. For example, is it only effects on humans (and what they care about) that are important, or might effects on the natural world require attention too?

Is promoting ethical consequences justified even when it requires ethical sacrifices along the way? Must there be a single unifying theory of ethics (such as the Utilitarian thesis that the right course of action is always the one that leads to the greatest happiness of the greatest number), or might there always be many different ethical values that pull a person in various directions?

As we enter into ethical debate and engage with these dilemmas on a personal and professional level, we may change our views or change our view of others. The real test though is whether, as we reflect on these matters, we change the way we act as well as the way we think. Socrates, the 'father' of philosophy, proposed that people will naturally do 'good' if they know what is right. But this point might only lead us to yet another question: *how do we know what is right?*

You

What are your ethical beliefs?

Central to everything you do will be
your attitude to people and issues around
you. For some people, their ethics are
an active part of the decisions they make
every day as a consumer, a voter or
a working professional. Others may think
about ethics very little and yet this does
not automatically make them unethical.
Personal beliefs, lifestyle, politics,
nationality, religion, gender, class or
education can all influence your ethical
viewpoint.

Using the scale, where would you place
yourself? What do you take into account
to make your decision? Compare results
with your friends or colleagues.

Your client

What are your terms?

Working relationships are central
to whether ethics can be embedded
into a project, and your conduct on
a day-to-day basis is a demonstration
of your professional ethics. The decision
with the biggest impact is whom you
choose to work with in the first place.
Cigarette companies or arms traders are
often-cited examples when talking about
where a line might be drawn, but rarely are
real situations so extreme. At what point
might you turn down a project on ethical
grounds and how much does the reality
of having to earn a living affect your ability
to choose?

Using the scale, where would you place
a project? How does this compare to your
personal ethical level?

01 02 03 04 05 06 07 08 09 10

01 02 03 04 05 06 07 08 09 10

Your specifications
What are the impacts of your materials?

In relatively recent times, we are learning that many natural materials are in short supply. At the same time, we are increasingly aware that some man-made materials can have harmful, long-term effects on people or the planet. How much do you know about the materials that you use? Do you know where they come from, how far they travel and under what conditions they are obtained? When your creation is no longer needed, will it be easy and safe to recycle? Will it disappear without a trace? Are these considerations your responsibility or are they out of your hands?

Using the scale, mark how ethical your material choices are.

Your creation
What is the purpose of your work?

Between you, your colleagues and an agreed brief, what will your creation achieve? What purpose will it have in society and will it make a positive contribution? Should your work result in more than commercial success or industry awards? Might your creation help save lives, educate, protect or inspire? Form and function are two established aspects of judging a creation, but there is little consensus on the obligations of visual artists and communicators toward society, or the role they might have in solving social or environmental problems. If you want recognition for being the creator, how responsible are you for what you create and where might that responsibility end?

Using the scale, mark how ethical the purpose of your work is.

01 02 03 04 05 06 07 08 09 10

01 02 03 04 05 06 07 08 09 10

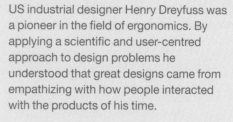

US industrial designer Henry Dreyfuss was a pioneer in the field of ergonomics. By applying a scientific and user-centred approach to design problems he understood that great designs came from empathizing with how people interacted with the products of his time.

In the 1930s, Bell Laboratories approached Dreyfuss to design 'the future of the telephone' as one of a small number of invited artists and craftspeople. Dreyfuss declined, suggesting that 'a telephone's appearance should be developed from the inside out.' The company disagreed, but returned to Dreyfuss several months later explaining that whilst the other artists offered interesting and original designs, they were all impractical.

Research began with Dreyfuss becoming the assistant of a telephone repairman so he could see what people really did with their phones. The result, launched in 1937, was the Bell 302, a rugged, easily repaired phone and the first to have all its circuitry in the base, without a separate ringer box. It had a metal finger dial with white porcelain numbered plate.

Improvements in electronics and plastics led to a redesign of the 302. Several years of research and testing by Dreyfuss led to the Model 500 being introduced in 1949. It improved upon several areas of design that had become problematic. The numbers on the porcelain dial plate wore off with use. The 500 put the numbers outside of the finger holes and moulded them into the black plastic rather than printing them on the surface. This enabled the user to see